THE
EXPEDITIONARY
MAN

Other Books by Rich Wagner

The Myth of Happiness

RICH WAGNER

THE
EXPEDITIONARY
MAN

The Adventure
a Man Wants,
the Leader
His Family Needs

ZONDERVAN®

ZONDERVAN.com/
AUTHORTRACKER
follow your favorite authors

 ZONDERVAN®

The Expeditionary Man
Copyright © 2008 by Rich Wagner

Requests for information should be addressed to:

Zondervan, *Grand Rapids, Michigan 49530*

Library of Congress Cataloging-in-Publication Data

Wagner, Rich.
    The expeditionary man : the adventure a man wants, the leader his family
needs / Rich Wagner.
        p.   cm.
    Includes bibliographical references.
    ISBN 978-0-310-27660-9
    1. Men (Christian theology) 2. Christian men—Religious life. I. Title.
BT703.5.W34   2008
248.8'42—dc22   2007045568

Scripture taken from the *Holy Bible, Today's New International Version*™. TNIV®.
Copyright © 2001, 2005 by International Bible Society. Used by permission of
Zondervan. All rights reserved.

Published in association with the literary agency of Alive Communications, Inc.,
7680 Goddard Street, Suite 200, Colorado Springs, CO 80920.

Interior design by Beth Shagene

Printed in the United States of America

08 09 10 11 12 13 • 22 21 20 19 18 17 16 15 14 13 12 11 10 9 8 7 6 5 4 3 2 1

To my friend Bob Geohle —
For you were there to encourage me when I started my
expedition.

CONTENTS

PREFACE

When I look back over the pages of this book, I am reminded of something novelist Thomas Wolfe once wrote: "We are the sum of all the moments of our lives—all that is ours is in them: we cannot escape or conceal it. If the writer has used the clay of life to make his book, he has only used what all men must." Indeed, when I first envisioned *The Expeditionary Man*, my mind was flooded with concepts and themes on biblical manhood. But when I sat down at my computer and began the task of writing, I soon realized that, in order to communicate my passion on this subject, I had to use "what all men must"—the experiences in my own life that have shaped me as a disciple, husband, father, and man.

This book turned into a most personal story, containing the clay of my life. My hope is that by sharing so openly with you, you'll discover that my path toward biblical manhood has not been an easy journey, but has stretched my marriage, my career, and even my faith to the breaking point. And, yet in spite of these challenges, I have discovered a life of adventure far greater than I could have ever imagined.

In addition to my own experiences, I also include several stories from other Christian men whom I have had the privilege to know over the past fifteen years in four different places that we have lived across the country. Except where I specifically note otherwise, all of these stories in the book are true. In most cases, however, I have changed the names and circumstances of the people to preserve confidentiality.

Finally, *The Expeditionary Man* focuses on the biblical role of the man in the home. Consequently, I deliberately avoid diving into the God-given role and responsibilities of a wife and mother. My omission is not in any way meant to slight or diminish the role of a woman in the household. No, that is a worthy subject for a different book.

RICH WAGNER
August 2007

CHAPTER 1

HARDWIRED FOR ADVENTURE

*I believe it is in our nature to explore,
to reach out into the unknown.
The only true failure would be
to not explore at all.*
—Ernest Shackleton

A man is hardwired for adventure. I see evidence of this truth everywhere. It's found in the films men love to watch and the sports they pursue. I spot it in the gleam of my friend's eye as he talks about his career change. And, more personally, I see it in the exploits that are written on my heart.

The question every Christian man wrestles with, however, is what to do with these desires. Is it possible for a man to pursue a life of adventure when he is married, raising kids, and paying a mortgage? How do I prioritize, a man asks himself, what I am driven to do with what I am responsible for?

Some men choose to live out their dreams, no matter the cost. Others stifle them in order to be a good family man. Many attempt to balance their pursuits with their responsibilities as husband and father. The problem is that when you look at the lives of men in the church today, nothing seems balanced at all. Too many Christian homes are falling apart. Too many youth are abandoning their faith as they hit college campuses. Too many Christian men are leading unfulfilled, mundane lives.

This battle of "adventure vs. duty" is brilliantly depicted in the Pixar film *The Incredibles*. The film chronicles the struggle of Bob Parr, a man who reluctantly gives up his livelihood as superhero Mr. Incredible and settles down into a normal suburban life. But after fifteen years, Parr's life has become one of monotony, boredom, and purposelessness. Working as an insurance agent, he spends his days cramped in a tiny cubicle, lost inside a faceless bureaucracy. Parr goes through the motions at work and zones out at home. In his glory days as Mr. Incredible, Bob Parr saved the world by capturing evil criminals. Now, in the words of his wife, his humdrum charge is to "save the world, one policy at a time."

Bob's thirst for adventure, however, can't be stomped out entirely, and it eventually surfaces again. Bob and his buddy Lucius (ex-superhero Frozone) go out every Tuesday night together. Their wives think they go bowling, but the two are actually listening to the police scanner so they can go fight criminals or help out in an emergency. Over time, Bob's "recreational" crime fighting ends up becoming his all-consuming focus when behind his wife's back he takes on a new assignment as a superhero. But when the mission goes awry, his family is nearly destroyed in the process.

Bob Parr tried to live a normal, quiet life. It was a life that his family and others expected of him. But, just like the real world, a man cannot live forever inside the walls of expectation. Adventure inevitably springs from the soul of a man.

Adventure in All Shapes and Forms

Let's face it: adventure just isn't the same nowadays. For nearly all of human history, this word signified real risk, genuine danger, and life-or-death competition. Uncharted lands were explored. A family's survival depended upon defeating enemies. And hard work was essential to surviving in a hostile environment. While most men wouldn't want to turn back the clock on the comfort and conveniences of the twenty-first century, they do grieve over what has been lost in a tame world. In fact, our situation today is reminiscent of a scene in the Jim Carrey film *The Truman Show*, when a young Truman eagerly tells his teacher that he wants to be another Magellan. Dousing all of his enthusiasm, she responds, "Oh, you're too late! There's nothing left to explore!" Like Truman, a man can feel as if he was born too late, that there's nothing left but a giant "Been There, Done That" sticker slapped on the earth.

God designed men to be resilient and adaptable creatures, however. Even if the grand discoveries of the past are now found only in history books, adventure is still alive and well in the heart of a man. In fact, the experience of the past century has shown that if a man can't find adventure in his daily life, he will manufacture it in his career, recreation, and, for Christians, a ministry.

Career

It's not just a job, it's an adventure. That slogan may be a tired, old U.S. Army advertising catchphrase, but it does get to the heart of what a man looks for in life. Every man wants an adventure for a career. Even the way in which we talk about business today reveals this reality. The corporate world is often portrayed in the media as a battleground for modern "warriors." Entrepreneurs are the heroic explorers, charting new waters in technology and the marketplace. Corporate pirates are the evil, greedy villains bent on world domination. Certainly in the Silicon Valley world I used to belong to, the passion for innovation in the early days of the Web had all the spirit of the inventors of yesteryear. My coworkers and I truly felt like we were living through something special, and we were all thrilled to be a part of it.

For a man spending most of his waking hours in this kind of environment, the idea of corporate warfare is intoxicating. The drive for a successful career is often too potent and seductive for him to resist. He is determined to win in the marketplace against his competition. He is motivated by the challenge of completing a major project on time and on budget. If he needs to, a man would work sixty hours a week or more to build his career and outshine his coworkers. None of these is an "adventure" in the classic sense. And, unless a man is a physician, his job is probably not a matter of life and death, but that doesn't really matter to him. Whether a man leads a Fortune 500 company, sells copiers, or crunches numbers for a living, his career can challenge, give purpose, and provide an identity for him.

Recreation

Not all men have jobs that challenge. Some men experience no adventure at all in their profession. Like Bob Parr in *The Incredibles*, they put in their time simply to bring home a paycheck. "I owe, I owe, so it's off to work I go" reads the old bumper sticker. For this man, adventure is something experienced on the weekends, manufactured through sports, hobbies, and other recreational activities. To make it through life, he gets enough of an "adventure fix" to make it through the drudgery or pressures of the work week. Some of the most popular pastimes include:

Outdoor recreation. Because so much of work today is performed behind a desk, outdoor activities and sports are one of the most coveted outlets for a man. The *Field & Stream* crowd goes fishing and hunting. The *Soldiers of Fortune* play paintball in the woods. The *Power Athletes* go mountain climbing, skiing, or cycling. Whatever the activity, outdoor physical activity somehow recaptures the age-old spirit of adventure and exploration in a man.

Digital entertainment. Within our technology-driven world, increasing numbers are letting their Xbox and PlayStation game consoles, televisions, and computers do the adventuring for them. While most people think of video games as a domain dominated by teenagers, the statistics reveal a far different reality. The average game player is a thirty-year-old male. Over four out of ten gamers are over the age of thirty-five, and a whopping 75 percent of all heads of households play regularly.

Youth sports. Coaching in youth sports is another magnet, particularly for ex-athletes desiring the thrill of competition that they once had in their school days. Why else would a grown man become passionate about the success or failure of his Little League team? Deep inside, there's something far more at stake for him than whether a bunch of elementary school kids win or lose a ballgame. To him, it's personal.

Spectator sports. Televised team sports may be the single most popular outlet for men. While the outdoor sportsman may scoff at the idea of real adventure while sitting on a couch in front of the television, the sports fan sees things differently. ESPN.com columnist Bill Simmons poignantly reveals why a spectator sport is so essential to so many men (emphasis mine):

> See, the best thing about following sports isn't the winning itself. It's everything that comes with the winning, namely, nationally televised games, extra playoff series to watch, extra phone calls and emails, extra tickets to try to get, and those mornings when you wake up and think, "Game day!!!!" (This explains why it's always slightly more agonizing when your team blows a conference championship – *they didn't just squander a chance to win the title, but you were so close to clinching another two-week stretch of being alive and everything that comes with it.*) When the Celtics sucked for almost all of the past 14 years, it wasn't the losing as much as the meaninglessness of it all. The team wasn't going anywhere. Nothing was happening. Nobody cared. Nobody could stop what was happening. Every day was more lackluster than the last one.

In a man's eyes, he is living out the highs and lows of competition, risk, and sense of belonging as he follows his favorite sports team.* When his team is riding high, he experiences, to use Simmons' words, that "stretch of being alive and everything that comes with it."

Movies. Men crave epic adventures at the cinema. These are the "guy films" that men love to watch over and over. One magazine defined the criteria of a guy film

---

* It's no coincidence that the invention and popularity of modern spectator sports has coincided with the increasing domestication of life. Men may have more free time to spend on recreation than they did two centuries years ago, but they have an increasing need for it as well.

as "violence trumps sex, war beats peace, and you better have a very good reason to oppose anything with Steve McQueen in it." In multiple polls on the most watched films by men, they are invariably adventure- or action-oriented films, including *Star Wars, Bladerunner, Die Hard,* and *The Lord of the Rings.*

Creative pursuits. Other men find adventure in creative activities, such as art, music, or writing. They experience a sense of purpose and fulfillment when they create or experience the creations of others. Think of C. S. Lewis, a lifelong academic and a man who never had an athletic bone in his body. Yet, when you read *The Chronicles of Narnia* or his space trilogy, you can tell that, inside his head, he too was living a life of genuine adventure.

Ministry

While some men may get involved in church ministries out of duty or sense of calling, others do so because it's a true adventure. Ministries give a man an opportunity to do activities he does best—problem solve, organize, lead, teach, and build. Not only does the work have purpose, but the nature of the work is fulfilling and a practical way to live out God-given gifts. Men who enjoy working with their hands can volunteer for a church remodeling project or a short-term missions construction trip. Leaders and teachers can serve in many positions around the church. Even men who are more reserved can have a role doing behind-the-scenes, handyman jobs. Being involved with a growing ministry can be an all-out thrill ride for a man. In our throwaway society, it is his chance to feel a part of something eternally significant.

PURSUITS

I have pursued adventure in most every way imaginable in my life. Back in my early twenties, I did what others around me thought was crazy—I organized and rode on two cross-country bicycle trips to raise money for a missions hospital in Haiti. After I got off the bike and started my marriage, I wasn't content to settle in one place for life. There was just too much of the world to see. So, during our twenties, my wife and I moved frequently, living in Washington, D.C., Colorado, the Midwest, and New England. Eventually, after we had children, I began to quench my thirst for adventure in my career. Driven to succeed in the high-tech world, I could always find a challenge that would keep me working long hours: inventing a software product, moving to a fast-rising Internet company in Silicon Valley, and then climbing up the corporate ladder. I worked hard to be a good husband and father, and I was involved in various church ministries. But, truth be told, my real passion was in my career.

However, as the years passed, I started to change. As I matured in my walk with Christ, I realized that in my drive to succeed in the workplace, I was neglecting my family at home. My marriage suffered. My boys were growing up quickly, and if I didn't make changes, I would miss out on their childhood. Over time, my passion for workplace success was superseded by the desire to be a good father and husband. But, in the process, I slowly began to lose the spirit of adventure that I had always had. Under the pressures of being a godly husband, raising three boys, and paying the bills, I gave up my aspirations and goals. I set out to do "the responsible thing." My thirst for adventure seemed incompatible with my calling at home; my only choice, I started to believe, was to give it all up.

I changed jobs. I moved from a dream role in a high-profile company to a downer of a job at Acme, Inc. On paper, the new position seemed ideal given my family focus: decent salary, no travel, and flexibility in telecommuting for much of the week. But I hated it. My role wasn't challenging or stimulating, and the company was going nowhere. I used to meet with industry movers and shakers; now I was working on a product no one cared about or had even heard of. My former office was bright, hip, and located in the heart of Silicon Valley; the new office was in a depressing brownstone that looked like something out of the *Mod Squad*.

My life started to resemble that of Bob Parr in *The Incredibles*. One scene of the film in particular captures the restlessness that stirred in my heart at that point of my life. Arriving home from work, Bob notices a little boy from the neighborhood staring at him as he gets out of his car. You see, the boy once saw Bob lift a car over his head, and so he regularly rides over on his tricycle to see more. When Bob asks the boy what he is waiting for, he responds, "I don't know. Something amazing, I guess." Bob sighs, "Me too, kid." Like Bob, I was waiting for something spectacular to happen in my life. I believed I was in the job God wanted me to be in at that point in my life, but I was convinced that there had to be more.

Years passed, and the desire for adventure swirled inside me once again. I was at a point in my career where I should have been most concerned with playing it safe: we had just moved into a new home, and my kids were entering their teen years. But common sense, I am discovering, can easily become an archenemy of following Jesus

Christ. Oswald Chambers, the Scottish preacher and author of *My Utmost for His Highest*, explains, "The temptation is to yield to ordinary common sense rather than wait for God to fulfill his purpose. God's order comes to us through the haphazard." Feeling led by God, I exchanged my safe, salaried career for a long shot at writing books for a living. But, this time around, I was determined to keep my aspirations in line with my family priorities.

GOING SOLO

It's been four years since that decision point in my life. Looking back today, what is more striking to me than the actual decision I made is how I made it: I was defining adventure purely in solo terms. Adventure, for me, was what I wanted to do with *my* career, *my* ministry, and *my* hobbies. My dreams were personal quests: to be a full-time Christian author, to launch a new discipleship ministry, to ride my bike across the United States again, to climb Mount Everest. Today, as I talk with other men, I realize that I am not alone in my solo quests for adventure.

Solo climbing is a type of mountaineering that involves going up a trail or cliff unsupported, not belayed by anyone else. Many consider it the ultimate mountain-climbing test. Requiring skill, stamina, and self-reliance, the challenge is entirely personal; it's a man versus a mountain. If you compare a man's outlook on life to a mountain ascent, a man tends to think like a solo climber. This teeth-clenched single-mindedness—whether it is on a mountain or in an office—is second nature to any man.

Consider, for example, John Eldredge's challenge at the close of *Wild at Heart*: "If you had permission to do what you really want to do, what would you do?... What is written on your heart? What makes you come alive?" Every man I've talked to who has read his book always answers Eldredge's question in solo terms. Take, for example, my friend Marty. His passion is to quit his sales job and enter full-time ministry. Robert, on the other hand, wants to launch a new company based on an invention he developed. My buddy Don is driven to start a new twentysomething outreach program at his church. No man I've encountered thinks of his family as being integral to the adventure he is seeking. Adventure is "out there" over the horizon; family is back at home. In fact, when thinking of his family, a man is usually gauging the negative impact that the pursuit of his dreams will have on his wife and children.

Seinfeld's George Costanza expresses the compartmentalizing that can take place in a man's life when his adventures are kept separate from his family. In the "Pool Boy" episode, George is stressed when his fiancée wants to hang around with his longtime circle of friends. Up until this point, George has successfully divided his life into Relationship George and Independent George. Now he's terrified at the prospect of having these two worlds collide. In desperation, he exclaims, "If Relationship George walks through this door, he will kill Independent George. A George divided against itself cannot stand!"

Some men share George's fear and will do anything to prevent their worlds from colliding. A second group of men give up altogether on the idea of adventure being compatible with family responsibilities. A final group attempts to balance these competing priorities. I call these three responses the Rugged Individualist, the Expectations Guy, and the Balanced Man.

The Rugged Individualist

A man can develop such a passion for pursuing adventure in his life that he becomes consumed by it, leaving his family behind in the process. Maybe he turns into a workaholic. Or perhaps he spends all his free time in a ministry or a hobby. The Rugged Individualist gives lip service to his family and may genuinely desire to be a good husband and father. But, deep down, a family feels like deadweight for a man who wants to pursue solo adventures.

The legendary Ernest Shackleton is the poster child of the Rugged Individualist. An arctic explorer, Shackleton is most remembered for his brilliant leadership during the ill-fated *Endurance* expedition to the South Pole in 1914 – 16. During the voyage, the ship that Shackleton and his crew were on became trapped in the ice and eventually sank. For nearly two years, Shackleton kept his team working together over ice, land, and sea, overcoming countless death-defying encounters, and enabling every member of his crew to survive the ordeal. For his mastery of survival and leadership skills, Shackleton is held up by many as one of the greatest heroes of our time. Even in Christian circles he is often hailed as a model leader of men.

Yet, in spite of his legendary skills, Shackleton was a lousy husband and father. He loved his family, but he was a restless spirit at home. After his *Endurance* expedition, he attempted a normal life back in England. It didn't take. Shackleton longed for another expedition, and within a few years, left again for Antarctica. "I suppose I'm just good as an explorer and nothing else," confessed Shackleton in a recent biopic film. Shackleton meant well, but his drive for adventure caused him to all but abandon his family in the process.

A man doesn't need to travel to the South Pole, however, to neglect his family in pursuit of individual fulfillment. He can just as easily do it while sleeping under the same roof.

The Expectations Guy

Other men, motivated by burden, responsibility, or earnest dedication to their family, feel as if they have no other choice but to suppress their desire for adventure. They focus instead on simply being a good husband and father. This man lives out his life based on other people's expectations, whether it is those of his wife, his church, or even (what he perceives as) God himself.

You see this in the movie *Before Sunset*, a story about two one-time lovers, Jesse and Celine, who lose touch with each other and meet back up a decade later. In their conversation, Jesse tells Celine about his unhappy marriage, prompting Celine to ask him why he got married in the first place. Jesse responds, "I had this idea of my *best self*, you know, and I wanted to pursue that even if it might have been overriding my *honest self*.... [Love] is ultimately the simple action of committing yourself, you know, meeting your responsibilities is what matters." But, by the end of the film, it becomes apparent that Jesse's "honest self" is winning out over his "best self."

A man's decision to put his family first is honorable and a demonstration of his spiritual leadership. However, like Mr. Incredible himself, he needs to be aware of the inherent dangers of living based on the opinions of others. Not only does a man risk wasting his talents and his calling (Matt. 25:14ff.), but he also can become a time bomb waiting to explode.

The Balanced Man

Within the church, movements like Promise Keepers and Man in the Mirror have had great success in challenging men to glorify God through their work, giving priority to their family, and serving Christ through a ministry. To many evangelical men today, "Balance" has become the mantra, the key to an effective Christian man's life—dividing time and priority between work, family, and a ministry.

The idea of a balanced approach certainly sounds good. The problem, however, is in actually pulling it off. Frankly, I am convinced that balance doesn't *really* work in the real world. Balance deals with a man's calendar, but it doesn't address matters of his heart. If a career or ministry is the primary way a man experiences adventure, then chances are strong that one of them will win his heart over in the long run.

In a tragic irony, dedicated Christian fathers can end up raising kids that hear all about the love of their Father in heaven but see an earthly dad far more devoted to and passionate about his career and ministry than his family. As a result, many of these kids become disillusioned as they get older and turn away from their Christian faith.

Bitter Pills

The fundamental problem with each of these three approaches to the "adventure versus duty" dilemma is that they artificially separate a man's drive for adventure from his family. Adventure becomes defined as what a man *wants* to do, while family is what he is *supposed* to do. Adventure is opportunity; family is obligation. "I'd love to go back to school and get a divinity degree," confessed a dear friend, "but my kids need to have food on the table." Throwing up his hands, he concluded, "I guess every man's gotta do what he's gotta do." My friend swallowed the bitter pill of broken dreams. And, in the process, he had started to view his family as a barrier and an obstacle to his true calling.

A SUMMIT ATTEMPT

At the start of this chapter, I raised the question that every man asks himself: *How do I prioritize what I am driven to do with what I am responsible for?* For years, I've wrestled with a biblical response. God designs the soul of a man for adventures and exploits. In doing so, God calls him to a life of discipleship in his career and ministry (Matt. 16:24; 28:19). Yet, if a man has a family, God also calls him to be a Christ-like husband (Eph. 5:23) and a spiritual leader and teacher of his children (Prov. 22:6). We seem bent on pitting these callings against each other, like boxers in a ring. But, as long as all of them are ordained by God, they should do more than just coexist, but actually thrive together. Each calling is meant to be a single thread, interwoven into the common fabric of a man's adventure.

Seen in this light, a man's life is not a solo climb at all. Instead, it is much like leading an Everest mountaineering expedition. Any summit attempt involves a team of climbers, several Sherpas (local hired climbers to carry supplies), and a team leader. The leader guides, protects, provides for, and, when necessary, sacrifices for his team. But, to the leader, these are more than responsibilities and chores; they are essential to the success of the expedition. An expeditionary leader can be consumed with reaching the summit, but he attains his goal by enabling his team to experience the same adventure.

When a man's life is an expedition, his family is no longer left behind at Base Camp while he makes a climb all by himself. Instead, his wife and children are participants accompanying him on a journey together. "Wherever you are, be all there," says missionary Jim Elliot. "Live to the hilt every situation you believe to be the will of God." When a man follows Elliot's challenge to "live to the hilt" in *every* calling of his life, then his home responsibilities no longer compete with his adventure; they help fulfill it. In fact, a man pursuing dreams by himself now resembles an expeditionary leader who brazenly leaves his team en route to the summit and makes his way on his own.

This book is about becoming an Expeditionary Man. It's the kind of man I want to become. I've certainly not reached the summit with my family. But the five of us are outfitted with climbing gear and gradually making our way up the mountain together. En route, however, I am discovering more and more about the true ownership of the climb: it's God's expedition, not my own. As such, I've had to realign my ideas of adventure to stay on his path up the mountain. Oswald Chambers puts it like this, "I realize more and more that if we are not to forego the interests of his cross we must forego a great many other interests and how you will go, counting Christ worthy of the cost."

When a man's kids are growing up in the home, I am convinced that he cannot act upon his career and ministry aspirations in the same way as he is free to during other seasons of his life. He foregoes them. Career ambitions are placed on hold. Ministries are limited for a time. After all, a man's primary mission field is his family; it's not the outside world. His adventures must, therefore, be fully consistent with that calling, just like an expeditionary leader orients his entire venture around the climbing team.

This realignment can be tough for a man because it means foregoing some of what naturally drives and motivates him. It also runs smack against what society—and even the church—expects of a man. But a quick read of Jon Krakauer's bestseller *Into Thin Air* will tell you that any Everest expedition led by a man with mixed agendas is doomed to failure. We shouldn't be surprised when the same setbacks and even disasters occur inside Christian homes.

"You are my greatest adventure," Bob Parr tells his family in the climax of *The Incredibles*. That line is more than lip service for the Expeditionary Man. It is part of God's perfect design for him. When a man lives out God's expedition rather than his own, not only will he raise spiritually healthy kids and have an ever-growing marriage, but he will also experience the godly adventure for which he so desperately yearns.

PART 1

CLIMBING SOLO

I dare do all that may become a man;
Who dares do more is none.
— Shakespeare, *Macbeth*

Everyone wants to save the world
But no one will take the blame
And when will we learn
The end result of our negligence
— Jonah33, "Father's Song"

CHAPTER 2

PUSHED AND PULLED

I cannot tell you how [Everest] possesses me.
— George Mallory, British mountaineering legend

I clicked the Start button on my work computer to shut it down. It was my last official action in my role as vice president, and I could not escape the irony of those familiar Microsoft Windows commands, *Start > Shut Down.* For in starting a new adventure in my life, I was shutting down a twelve-year-old career in software development in the process.

I packed up the rest of my belongings in my desk, but there was not much left. A coffee mug, some papers from HR, my last paycheck, and a handful of backup CDs. I'd been planning this move for months, so the odds and ends easily fit into my briefcase. With my corporate keepsakes in hand, I did a final walk-through of the office, ending at my boss's door to say good-bye. Both of us looked at each other with an almost quizzical expression — a mixture of empathy and excitement over the path the other was taking. He was trying to sell his fledging company to a suitor in Silicon Valley; I was going out on my own as a full-time Christian author. Both ventures seemed highly speculative at best.

My pace was abnormally fast as I left the office and went down two flights of stairs toward the front door. An adrenaline rush perhaps. More likely, it was some irrational fear of being grabbed at the last moment and sucked back into the corporate world. It was hard not to think of that scene in *The Lord of the Rings* where Gandalf, just when you think he is safe, is suddenly pulled by the whip of the Balrog into the abyss.

I got into my car and headed home. Far away from the reaching grip of any corporate Balrog, I could now relax—my adventure, some five years in the making, was officially starting! Ever since the dotcom boom of the 1990s, I had been growing increasingly tired of working in an environment in which all of my creativity, dedication, and hard work would produce something that became obsolete in a year's time. I was ready for something more. I had prayed and fasted for a chance at making it to this summit—and now here I was.

The idea of starting over in my vocation was sobering and terrifying. After all, I had just turned thirty-seven. I had a wife, three boys, and a newly built home. That fear was dwarfed, however, by my sense of purpose, conviction, and the joy of living out a longtime dream. But I would soon discover that not everything was as it appeared to be.

Mountaineers tell of false summits that a climber can reach as he ascends a peak. From the view below, the crest that the climber is scaling appears to be the top of the mountain. However, upon reaching it, he discovers it is actually a false summit; the actual peak is much higher up.

In launching my authoring career, I thought I had reached the mountaintop where God wanted me to be. But after only a few months, I began to realize that responding to God's call had far different implications than what I had ever dreamt. I was not on the summit after all. He had something else in mind farther up, farther in.

But perhaps I am getting a little ahead of myself. My story of becoming an Expeditionary Man has roots several years earlier in my life on a much darker mountain . . .

PUSHED
FROM THE INSIDE

Mount Everest is a colossal, three-sided pyramid rising up from the other great peaks of the Himalayas. Its three massive faces are not particularly steep or jagged to climb. In fact, as a technical challenge, it is not nearly as difficult as Annapurna or K2. But more than any place on earth, the 29,035-foot summit of Everest is the stuff of legend and lore. *The Rooftop of the World. The Third Pole.* Everest is a breathtaking reminder of the creative power of God and even seems to mimic the personality of the God of the Old Testament—awesome and glorious, but also jealous, demanding, and occasionally vengeful.

Over the past hundred years, no place on Earth has sparked as many dreams of adventure as Mount Everest. Mountaineer Thomas F. Hornbein recalls being mesmerized by a blurred picture of Everest in an obscure geography book years before Edmund Hillary led the first successful conquest in 1953. He said, "Dreams were key to the picture . . . I was sure that mine about Everest was not mine alone; the highest point on earth, unattainable, foreign to all experience, was there for many boys and grown men to aspire toward."

Decades later, Doug Hansen was one of those dreamers Hornbein was referring to. Doug was not your typical Everester: he was a forty-five-year-old postal worker from Seattle, not a professional climber. Prior to his first Everest attempt, he had no actual experience on any of the world's elite peaks. Truth is, Doug was an ordinary man with an extraordinary dream. *Someday. Somehow. If I can just get the opportunity*, Doug would say to himself, *I know I can make it to the top of Everest.*

Doug knew the odds were stacked against him, but he was relentless in the pursuit of his objective. He spent over fifteen years training and climbing in the Pacific Northwest. He wasn't an expert by any means, yet he gradually developed the physical endurance and mental toughness needed for an Everest bid. Regardless of how well he could perform physically, however, Doug faced a Himalayan-sized financial hurdle as well: the cost. The price tag for joining a commercial expedition to Everest was a hefty $65,000. The exorbitant fee normally makes such expeditions the domain of wealthy enthusiasts and climbing professionals, but the working-class Hansen was not deterred. To finance his trip, Doug began working the night shift at the post office and then moonlighting during the day doing construction jobs. It took years to raise the money, but by 1995, he had finally earned enough. Doug signed up with Adventure Consultants, a New Zealand firm led by a renowned mountain guide named Rob Hall.

Like most other modern commercial expeditions, Rob's team used a military-like "siege" strategy of attacking the mountain. Using this technique, the team establishes a Base Camp at around 17,500 feet, where the team members begin to acclimatize to the altitude. Sherpas travel ahead to establish a series of four camps (named Camp 1, Camp 2, Camp 3, and Camp 4) approximately two thousand feet apart from each other. At each camp, the Sherpas stockpile food, oxygen tanks, cooking fuel, and shelter that will be used by the full team when they arrive. The team then progressively climbs up to these different camps and back down over successive weeks to acclimatize to the higher altitudes. Finally, when the team is ready physically and the weather looks favorable, the team members move to Camp 4 at 26,000 feet to position themselves for a summit bid.

During the weeks of acclimatization, Rob Hall and the others took an instant liking to the friendly, good-natured Doug. Experienced guides, who often roll their eyes at "Gumbys" (novice climbers), found themselves respecting his work ethic and climbing passion. All wanted Doug to fulfill his lifelong dream of reaching the top.

The "day of days" arrived. The team plan was excruciating—some nine to ten hours up, and five to six hours back down to the camp. It was also precise. Every summit attempt of Everest is a life-or-death encounter against a fickle clock—battling constant fatigue, unpredictable physical and mental problems caused by the high altitude, and fierce blizzards that chronically swallow the summit. The mortality rate of the mountain bears out the danger: approximately one in ten Everest climbers are killed in their attempt. As a result, teams must get up and down as fast as possible in order to survive. If a climber does not turn around by early afternoon, he risks getting stranded and dying of exposure before he is able to descend to safety.

Rob's team departed Camp 4 in the dark hours of the night. But it wasn't long before Doug realized he just wasn't feeling right. He kept going, but each individual step upward became a battle—take a step … pause … take a breath … pause … take another step. His mind also started to play games. *Is the summit just ahead? Where is this path leading to? Why am I breathing from this oxygen tank?*

Realizing that Doug was in trouble, one of the guides began shouting at Doug over and over to keep him moving along. Eventually, in spite of his problems, Doug and the other team members were able to reach a place known as the "south summit," just 330 vertical feet below the summit top.

Three hundred and thirty feet. Back on sea level, that amount seems tantalizingly close. Peyton Manning needs a mere two minutes to lead his team that distance from one end zone to the other. A world-class hurdler can do even better—hurdling some 110 meters in just over twelve seconds. But the last 330 vertical feet atop Mount Everest is real estate not so easily conquered. Since it re-quired at least two hours of climbing, Rob was gravely concerned about the rapidly deteriorating weather condi-tions and treacherous snow just above them. As difficult a call as it was, Rob turned the group around and returned to Camp 4.

Doug made it back safely to the camp, but he was crushed. Perhaps a line from *Field of Dreams* best de-scribes Doug's disappointment: "It would kill some men to get so close to their dream and not touch it … they'd consider it a tragedy." Not being able to walk up those last 330 steps was, in his mind anyway, a genuine tragedy. "The summit looked *sooooo* close," Doug lamented later. "Believe me, there hasn't been a day since that I haven't thought about it."

Rob Hall knew he'd made the right call, but felt terrible about Doug's near miss. In fact, he soon promised Doug that if he would come back next year, he would definitely get him to the top. Rob even offered Doug a significant discount off the normal fee if he tried again. As you might expect, it didn't take much prodding for Doug to take Rob up on his offer and try again to reach the top of Everest in 1996. Conquering Everest was in his blood.

Doug Hansen is not unique. Every man has his own version of the "climbing bug" that can push him up mountains, into corporate boardrooms, on short-term mission trips, or onto the couch watching sports on weekends. In fact, Doug's single-mindedness toward Mount Everest reminds me of the passion I had for my career soon after I graduated from college. Like Doug, I was a tenacious go-getter. "The relentless pursuit of perfection" was the slogan of the automobile maker Lexus during that time. I claimed that phrase as my own and used it as motivation for everything I did.

As a fresh college graduate, however, my aspirations were not exactly in line with my experience. It took me six months just to get an entry-level job. And the position I wound up in was not much of a dream role at all. I was doing drudge work, was earning a paltry salary, and had no advancement possibilities. Undeterred, I worked my tail off anyway. I plugged away in these types of low-level roles for a few years, all the while dreaming and scheming for something more. *If I can just get an employer to give me an opportunity*, I told myself, *I know I will succeed.*

After I gained more experience, I finally got the opportunity that I had always been looking for with a fast-growing software company. I had more responsibility than I ever had before and a chance to grow my career. As projects came in, I attacked them with a siege mentality—battling the deadlines and technical hurdles with a relentless attitude. Any success I enjoyed only gave me an adrenaline rush for more. I didn't care how many hours I worked or how many all-nighters I had to put in. I had finally arrived, and I was going to do great things. Conquering the software world was in my blood.

PULLED
BY THE OUTSIDE

The "climbing bug" has always been a driving force deep inside a man that, if left unchecked, can push a man away from his family. My story only cracks the surface. A peek into the private lives of many explorers and inventors of the world attest to this fact. Folk hero Davy Crockett's life of adventure and travel came at a cost—he was married three times. Frontiersmen Simon Kenton and Daniel Boone would leave home for months at a time without any word to their families as to their return. In fact, Boone was gone on an adventure so long that when he came back, he was more than a little surprised to discover that his wife had given birth to his brother's son.

There is, however, also a force from outside a man that pulls him further away from his family—the norms and expectations of our culture. The very structure of our society and economy rips a man from his family and tells him that fulfillment is found outside the home. There are few expectations, even within the church itself, for a man to be a constant presence and hands-on guide for his family. In fact, consider the following five statements that our culture affirms as true:

- A man's place is at the office.
- A man is defined by what he does.
- A healthy family is one that encourages and fosters personal goals and accomplishments.
- A husband and wife are interchangeable parts in leading a family.
- "Someone else" is better equipped to teach a man's children.

When I read these statements, I immediately think of this line from *The Truman Show*: "We accept the reality of the world with which we are presented. It's as simple as that." I am convinced that we accept these five great cultural myths without debate. But when a man buys into these myths and lives according to them, he ends up creating an ever larger gap between his family and himself. Let's take a look at each of these misconceptions.

A man's place is at the office. During the week, the average man spends the majority of his schedule either at work or commuting there. Given the amount of time he is at the office, it is natural for him to begin to treat it as "his place." His economic needs are met there. His social needs for collegiality, community, and friendship are often met at the office. His personal and emotional goals are also achieved at work. For many men, the office is where he is in his element, doing what he does best.

I think of the scene in the film *Sabrina* in which the main character (Sabrina) is talking with Linus Larrabee, a Donald Trump-like corporate mogul, about work and home. Linus tells her, "Listen, I work in the real world with real responsibilities."

"I know you work in the real world and you're very good at it," Sabrina responds. "But that's work. Where do you live, Linus?" For millions of men today, the answer to that question is their office.

A man did not always find his identity and purpose at work. Before the mid-1800s, the average man farmed for a living. I used to envision an old-time farmer working away in the fields all by himself twelve hours a day, six days a week. But as I researched the topic, I discovered that farming wasn't a solo activity for men at all. Rather than doing this job by himself, he acted much more like the CEO of a family corporation. All the members of the household worked together to produce food and income for the family. Along the way, a man taught his children how to plant and harvest crops, fish and hunt, handle livestock, and so on. Except for the occasional sailors, soldiers, and bureaucrats, even men who didn't farm had a family business at or near his house. As a result, from sunrise to sundown, a man was in regular and often constant contact with his family.

All of this changed, however, with the Industrial Revolution. As men left their farms to work in factories, every aspect of their lives was transformed. A man's schedule changed. He now found himself spending most of his waking hours at a factory instead of around home. His priorities shifted; he became less concerned with running his family and more preoccupied with his job. His psyche changed. Personal, social, and economic goals were increasingly fulfilled at the workplace, not at home.

Not surprisingly, a man's influence over his family began to dwindle. Being around the home 24/7, the homesteading father was a constant, steady influence over his family. Christian fathers, in particular, used this as a time to teach their children vocationally, educationally, and, most important, spiritually. But in this brave new world, the wife gradually became, for all practical purposes, the head of the family. A man had little energy for such activities anymore after being gone all day. In his book *Iron John*, Robert Bly writes about how that attitude carries over to the present day:

> What the father brings home today is usually a touchy mood, springing from powerlessness and despair mingled with longstanding shame and the numbness peculiar to those who hate their jobs ... when a father, absent during the day, returns home at six, his children receive only his "temperament" and not his "teaching." If the father is working for a corporation, what is there to teach? He is reluctant to tell his son what is really going on. The fragmentation of decision-making in corporate life ... the prudence, even cowardice, that one learns from bureaucracy—who wants to teach that?

It's no exaggeration to say that the Industrial Revolution led to a Manhood Devolution. Manhood became more and more about income generation, less and less about sacrificial leadership. "For the first time," notes author Weldon Hardenbrook, "it was socially and morally acceptable for men *not* to be involved with their families." Not surprisingly, the stereotype of the out-of-touch, clueless dad was formed during this period. "While the American man rules in the business world, his wife rules at home," quips a Paris newspaper article from 1912. This trend continues today, of course. In the media, a father is constantly depicted as incompetent, prone to giving bad advice, and standing on the sidelines of the family.

While the "clueless father" may be a stereotype, the sad truth is that many men really are, to varying degrees, on the periphery of their families. Only a handful of men nowadays are a constant presence and influence in their households during the work week—even those who telecommute regularly. Because of their jobs, the idea of hands-on leadership seems like an impossibility to a man. Various studies show a father spending twenty to sixty minutes daily with their kids. Even worse, another study indicated that the average teenager growing up in a Christian home spends just two minutes per day in conversation with his or her father. To top it off, one in four of these same Christian teens say that they have *never* had a conversation with their father that focused on their interests or needs.

A man is defined by what he does. The social and economic changes over the past 250 years not only shifted a man's attention to the workplace, but it also changed the way a man views himself. For much of human history, a man's identity and security came from his family. In ancient and medieval times, a man would be introduced to others as the "son of so-and-so," a sign of respect to him because of his family ties. In fact, perhaps the greatest insult you gave a man from ancient Israel was to say that he had no family roots.

Today's world could hardly be more different. A man's self-identity is wrapped up almost entirely in what he does. His career gives him a sense of self-worth and defines the kind of man he sees himself as being. Society embraces the self-made individual. Other men may not be as career focused, but their self-identity remains tied to something else they do—be it a hobby, sport, or ministry at church.

Consider, for example, the typical introduction that takes place between two men at church or a social event. They'll introduce themselves to each other, and then the conversation will inevitably turn to a mutual exchange of "And what do you do?" I certainly fall into that trap all the time.

The link between a man's self-identity and his career is perhaps best seen when that career is taken away. Studies tell of the high number of men who die within a year of their retirement, unable to cope in a world without a job to go to. Or, when a man is laid off, financial insecurity is often dwarfed by the "identity theft" that the layoff triggers.

A healthy family is one that encourages and fosters personal goals and accomplishments. The typical family from centuries past was closely dependent on each other relationally, emotionally, and economically. Of course, I am not so naïve to think that men were perfect leaders of the families in the "good ol' days." But at the same time, the reality was that even in less than ideal circumstances, the lives of family members were invested in each other in a way we do not grasp today.

When a man headed off to work, this fabric of unity slowly began to unravel. Mom and the kids adjusted to the father's absence and started to get along without him. Then, in the twentieth century, as women began entering the workplace in large numbers, children grew increasingly independent from both their father and mother. Kids began to identify more and more with their peer groups and less and less with their siblings and parents. When going to social events and recreational activities, for example, teens began expecting to go with their friends, not their families. The upshot of it all is that each family member now had their own personal agenda and spent little time or energy on concerns of the entire family.

Looking around today, I can easily see the end result of this change. The postmodern family is less a single cohesive unit than it is an affiliation of free agents, each with their own individual goals and pursuits. Consider the lifestyle of the Smiths, a typical Christian family of four living in the twenty-first century. While Joe Smith is at the office, his wife, Brenda, is either working herself or managing the home. Their daughter, Sally, goes to the local high school, while their son, Johnny, attends a special honors program across town. Struggling in math, Sally goes to a tutor three afternoons weekly; Johnny has violin lessons on the other two afternoons. Both kids play intramural sports at their respective schools on Saturdays —volleyball for Sally and soccer for Johnny. Sally attends high school youth group on Mondays, while Johnny goes to the junior high youth group on Wednesdays.

Sally and Johnny's parents run themselves ragged and the family has little or no time together, but culture views this model as perfectly normal and healthy. In fact, the more parents aim to buck this trend and keep their family together by homeschooling or limiting extracurricular sports and activities, they are often looked down upon as being antisocial. *They're depriving their children*, onlookers scowl. In truth, when we go along unquestionably with society's norms, it is the family who is being deprived—of each other.

A husband and wife are interchangeable parts in leading a family. For much of human history, the concept of a patriarchal leadership of a family was not only accepted, it was a given. A father was the head of the household, responsible for discipline, teaching, and management. Patriarchy comes from two Latin words: *patria* ("from father") and *arche* ("to rule"). It literally means a "family ruler," the mere uttering of which sounds offensive to modern ears.

Our culture—and a surprising number of people in the church—believe that a man's leadership role in the family has nefarious implications. "Male-led" automatically means "male-dominated." The idea of servant leadership as expressed in Ephesians 5:25–28 is dismissed out of hand. When we write off the special leadership role that a man can bring to the home, Mom and Dad become interchangeable parts. Mom can lead or Dad can lead—just so someone does it. As a result of this backlash, many men simply retreat into their own private world. They become Provider Dads, relegating the responsibility of leading their families to their wives.

Someone else is best equipped to teach a man's children. The concept of a "teaching father" is almost unheard of within the church and larger society. Think back to my Smith family example. Joe is probably content that he is able to manage his children's education, sporting, musical, and spiritual teaching, even if all of the running around does make life hectic at home. While the Smiths are, in many ways, a portrait of the postmodern family, notice what has happened: the kids are going from one specialist to another during the week in an effort to expand their knowledge and train their skills—school teachers, honors teachers, tutors, music teachers, coaches, Sunday school teachers, and youth pastors.

The net effect on the role of the parents is that they can become reduced to being nothing but glorified logistics coordinators—responsible for getting the kids from one specialist to another. The role reduction is a self-fulfilling prophecy that impacts both kids and parents. As time goes on, the children see their father less as a leadership figure because the authorities in their lives for much of the week are other people. In addition, because the father relinquishes so much authority, he no longer views himself as being responsible (*It's their job, not mine*), or he develops an inferiority complex (*They're better at it than I am*), or he looks at it pragmatically (*As long as the job gets done, I don't cares who does it*).

This was not always the case. Before the Industrial Revolution, most fathers actively participated in many aspects of their children's education. Working alongside their kids during the day, they regularly taught them vocational skills. Many fathers were also involved at some level in teaching music and academic subjects. Finally, before the age of youth group ministries, a Christian man provided biblical instruction to lay a sound theological framework for his children. But as men went off to factories and offices, a father's involvement in their children's education became rarer and rarer, particularly as free public education began to sweep the country in the nineteenth century. Around the same time, the church soon became the primary location for receiving biblical education rather than the home.

Few Christian men today see the need to be anything other than overseer in their children's education and basic Christian teaching. Even in the homeschooling community, male involvement is rare. *The mother is the teacher, the father is the principal* is the ubiquitous model.

Ever since the days of Adam, men have struggled with the "climbing bug"—the desire to do great things in the world at nearly any cost. But this instinctive drive toward adventure was often counterbalanced by the culture around them. Society helped bring the wayward man back in line with his responsibilities at home. But today's man no longer has cultural pressure that brings him back to the middle. With a culture devoted to individualism, personal liberties, and private goals, I am convinced that the twenty-first century is the most challenging period in human history for a Christian man to focus on his family.

Tossed around like a sailboat on a stormy sea, a man is pushed by his longing for adventure and pulled by a culture that expects him to find himself in the workplace. It's not surprising, then, that so many Christian men experience disasters when they go with this current.

LOSING PERSPECTIVE

Doug Hansen may have fallen 330 feet short of the Everest summit in 1995, but, as everyone expected, he was back the next year on Rob Hall's team with even more confidence and motivation. *This is my year,* he convinced himself. But as the twelve-person team began their training, Doug didn't seem nearly as strong this time around. During an acclimatizing trip to Camp 3, Doug developed a frozen larynx and found himself completely unable to talk. He initially feared that the trip would be over for him because of the injury. However, he was able to recover from this ailment before the summit attempt. As the team left for Camp 4, readying for the final push to the top, he was hopeful that his physical problems were behind him. But by the time he arrived at the camp, Doug was in poor shape. Teammate Beck Weathers recalls, "He looked like he'd been worked over with an ice ax. Even more so than the rest of us, he hadn't been feeding and watering and resting the machine that has to carry you up the hill." Despite his weakened state, Doug vowed to continue on anyway. *I refuse to let this stop me.*

The summit day arrived. However, after a few hours into the summit climb, fellow climber Jon Krakauer recalls that Doug stepped out of line. He told Jon that he had decided to quit and turn around to descend to Camp 4. *I just don't have the goods this year,* Doug thought to himself. However, before he started back, team leader Rob Hall came over and talked to him. No one knows exactly what was said, but Doug decided to continue on.

As the hours passed, the team began stretching out in a long line up to the summit. Doug fell to the rear, prompting Rob to go back to help him out. As in the previous year, 2:00 p.m. was the stated turnaround time. However, as the deadline passed, Rob and Doug mysteriously continued climbing toward the summit, even as other team members were working their way back down. Progress was painfully slow for the two. 2:30 ... 3:00 ... 3:30 ... and finally 4:00 p.m. passed before Rob and Doug reached the peak. The duo had little time to celebrate because, by this critically late hour, massive storm clouds were overtaking the summit.

Only moments later, they were in a complete whiteout. The two descended to the top of a forty-foot-high cliff known as the Hillary Step, where Doug collapsed and was unable to continue on his own strength. Rob would not leave Doug, but could not revive him either. They were trapped in a true "no-man's-land." As the night rolled on, Base Camp received periodic transmissions from Rob. *I am trying to get Doug to descend,* he radioed. However, by

5:00 a.m. the following morning, Rob reported the terrible news that Doug was gone. To this day, no one knows whether Doug froze to death or fell off the edge trying to descend. Hours later, Rob himself died just short of the south summit.

When I read about this tragedy, it's easy for me to pounce on the decision of Doug and Rob to continue after the 2:00 p.m. deadline and to be outraged over the waste of it all. After all, is any summit attempt worth risking your life? But no sooner do I do that when Matthew 7:3 ("Why do you look at the speck of sawdust in someone else's eye and pay no attention to the plank in your own eye?") hits me like a brick. I realize that others could easily say the same thing to me about a decision I made years ago. *What a waste! Is a career worth risking your marriage and family?* they may have thought. And they would be right, because my passion and enthusiasm for my career almost had tragic and devastating consequences.

It all started a few months into the software job I waited so long to get. In my desire to succeed, I completely lost perspective on work and family priorities. I am convinced it was a spiritual attack, but I certainly was a willing participant in the rebellion. My life became all about *my* goals and *my* desires. I was in pro form at work, but was an absentee father and husband at home. Not surprisingly, my new attitude didn't go over well with my wife, Kim. A rift soon developed over the amount of attention I was placing on my career. Kim resented my preoccupation with the office when we had three growing boys in the home. In turn, I became embittered over her lack of support for this opportunity that I had been awaiting patiently for so long. Weeks passed and the tension continued. I began to look at myself more and more as a solo climber. Kim, it seemed to me, was back at Base Camp seeking to prevent me from climbing any mountain at all.

With each passing week, I became more and more emotionally detached from home. The career/home tension was spilling over into other areas of our relationship. The issues Kim and I were dealing with were not easily swept under the rug. In fact, they were threatening the very fabric of our marriage. Oh, I had occasional reality checks, telling myself that I needed to turn around, regroup, and head in a different direction. However, just like Doug Hansen on his futile Everest climb, my perspective was skewed. My judgment was clouded in a haze of career aspiration and emotional confusion.

The work-versus-home battle left my life in a state of turmoil. My original dream had always been to be successful at work and to be a godly husband and father at home. But in my preoccupation with my career, I began to realize that I was betraying everything about who I thought I was. As time went on, I came to terms with my sin, repented, and gradually worked through the ordeal with Kim to restore our marriage.

When I look at Doug's tragedy and my near disaster, I am struck that ignorance played no part in either of our two crises. Instead, a mixture of adverse conditions and poor judgment became a recipe for disaster regardless of how invulnerable we believed ourselves to be. Long-time Mount Rainier guide Lou Whittaker has seen many climbers making the same tragic mistakes. His words are applicable for any man smitten with the "climbing bug":

> Lots of experienced mountaineers take chances and make mistakes. Most of them don't make mistakes

out of ignorance. They know what the consequences of their actions might be. They take a calculated risk and play the odds. Climbing Everest without oxygen is more dangerous than climbing with it. Climbing solo without backup and no equipment except two water bottles is sticking your neck way out. Some people like the added thrill of burning their bridges behind them. I call that *dumb mountaineering.* To me, there are enough risks out there already: lightning, storms, rock- and icefalls, avalanches, earthquakes, snow blindness, equipment failures, high-elevation sickness, frostbite, and sunburn. Why manufacture more?

By the grace of God and my wife, I survived my "dumb manhood." I avoided a possible disaster that could have ruined everything in my life. But as I look around at many other Christian homes, I see that the "climbing bug" remains a clear and present danger. The solo climbs of men create a fallout of disillusionment and resentment in the lives of their children. Just ask Adam and Kendra.

CHAPTER 3

Frostbitten Families

I've become so numb, I can't feel you there …
All I want to do is be more like me and be less like you.
—Linkin Park, "Numb"

"Can't we just elope?" Adam asked Kendra as they were looking at their summer calendar. It was a nonsensical question and he knew it.

No response.

"Vegas?" he tacked on to get a reaction.

"Go click your camera in Sudan by yourself if you want to do that," Kendra shot back.

"Okay, I admit Las Vegas is not my favorite place either," Adam grinned. Turning more serious, he said, "But it has got to be better than getting married at Grace Trinity. I don't want to set foot in that place on the most important day of our lives."

"Can't you just make it through one hour there?" Kendra asked. "I've dreamt of a big church wedding my whole—"

"—But why *my* home church?" Adam interrupted. "I thought tradition says it's supposed to be the bride's?"

"Come on, Adam. It has to be there. Africa is out of the question."

Adam and Kendra were seniors at Florida State University preparing for a busy spring—graduating in May and then getting married in June. According to their friends, the two were a perfect match. Though they grew up a half a world apart, they met early at college and quickly became kindred spirits. Both were outgoing and athletic and had a passion for traveling. Adam majored in photojournalism, while Kendra majored in journalism. Both idealists, they were ready to right the wrongs of the world with their camera and pen when they became freelance journalists after graduation.

The couple shared a similar background as well. Each was raised in a "model" Christian home, born again by sixth grade, and baptized soon after. By the end of their freshman year at Florida State, however, they both had left their childhood faith far behind.

Adam was the youngest son of Robert Michaels, an attorney for a Washington, D.C., law firm and chairman of the elder board at a growing suburban church. Robert was the prototype of a highly successful Christian businessman, the kind of person who was destined to be featured on the cover of *New Man* magazine. He possessed the trifecta coveted by every Christian man: *prominent at work, leader in his church, and devoted at home.* When others in the church went to the Michaels' home for Bible study or a dinner, they would comment on the peace and joy they felt there. *A little slice of heaven in worldly McLean* was the running yarn among friends.

But not everything was as it appeared to be in the

Michaels' household. Robert had a heart of gold to everyone who knew him, but he always seemed to be occupied with something other than his family. He was busy nearly every night of the week with an elders' meeting, a men's Bible study, a marriage support group he and his wife led, and half a dozen projects he had going on in his den. Robert was quick to challenge Adam in his Christian walk—*Did you do your devos today? Are you really living out your faith at school?*—but he spent little time one-on-one with his son. Truth is, by the time Adam was in his teens, it was clear that Robert had given his best years of fathering to Adam's older brothers, both of whom were long gone.

Every August, however, Robert always managed to take Adam on the church's annual father and son campout. It was during these outings that he would play catch-up with his son on spiritual matters, and Adam never failed to give the answers he thought his dad wanted to hear. By all appearances, Adam was doing just fine. He was well adjusted at school, active in his youth group, and leading the youth music team. At one of the campouts, he even talked with his dad about going into youth ministry someday.

Robert didn't realize, however, that Adam was a people pleaser—a "Golden Retriever" type as Christian counselor Gary Smalley puts it. He was always trying to earn his father's attention and approval through his "Christianese" talk and behavior. Soon after Adam the Golden Retriever went off to college, however, he wagged his tail for a new master. He became much more interested in earning approval from his college buddies and much less willing to be the perfect son that his dad expected him to be.

Kendra was raised as a missionary kid in Cote D'Ivoire,

West Africa. Since her parents, Glenn and Rachel Parker, left the States when Kendra was only four years old, the mission field was all she really knew growing up. When the Parker family arrived in Africa, they immediately felt pressure from the mission board to hit the ground running. There was just so much work to do. Given the trouble he had raising money, Glenn also felt an unspoken burden to have powerful headlines for his monthly newsletters to his financial supporters in the U.S. The pressure was not just on Glenn either; the mission board required missionary wives to do 50 percent of the work, leaving Rachel with little time to devote to her four daughters at home. Like most other missionaries in the area, the Parkers sent Kendra and her three sisters to Albert Academy, a boarding school about two hours away. The decision to board their daughters was tough, but it was all part of being in God's service, Glenn and Rachel concluded.

Most of Kendra's childhood memories centered on Albert Academy. In fact, her peers and teachers became far more of an influence than her parents ever were. As time went on, Kendra began to look on boarding school as "normal life" and had a difficult time adjusting when she was home during holiday breaks. With so much happening to her while at the academy, it seemed impossible to regain any degree of intimacy with her parents when she was with them. By the final years of high school, Kendra had given up even trying.

Inside their one-bedroom apartment, Adam and Kendra continued to plan their wedding ceremony.

"So why are you dreading going into Grace Trinity?" asked Kendra. "Feeling guilty?"

Adam shrugged off the question. *Grace Trinity it would be.* No more debate was necessary.

Kendra said, "Let's talk about the guest list."

"Hey, what about your parents? Think they'll fly over for the big event?"

"Of course," she responded. "They're taking a furlough this summer."

"And they'll really come? Even though you are marrying a prodigal?"

"Oh, they've made their opinion loud and clear, but they'll still be there."

"Funny. Since our first date, neither of us has said so much as a word about faith ... I'm curious—how exactly did an MK like you become a heathen like me?"

"I don't know if I left my faith so much as I've became numbed to the whole thing," Kendra sighed.

"Are you *ever* going to talk about what happened?"

Kendra shook her head and almost blew off the question. "Let's get back to work," she started to say. But the question gave her pause, as if it was the first time in a long while that she had thought about growing up back in Africa. Turning to Adam, she said, "You know, for as long as I can remember, I've always felt like I was less important than the work of God. My dad was constantly making short-term compromises at our expense. *Once I do this job, then I'll spend more time with you gals*, he would assure us. But it was all bull. He had no time during the eighteen months of language study in Switzerland. He had no time when we actually got to the mission field. Even when my sisters and I went off to school, he never had time for us on our break. The mission *always* came first to my parents."

"Sounds familiar," said Adam. "The only time I can remember Dad not working was on Christmas, Easter, and maybe Thanksgiving. I think he felt a constant pressure to be on top of everything at work and at church. He just didn't feel that same pressure to be a real father at home."

"But there was one night in particular that always stood out to me," Kendra said. "It was the last night of Christmas break during my junior or senior year. Jenna, she must have been ten at the time, had been planning a family game night all break. She insisted on doing everything —cooking the meal, organizing the games, making decorations, the works. Wouldn't you know it, right before supper, Dad got a call to run over to the next town to deal with a power outage at a new clinic he had just opened. Since he was the lone American around, I am sure he believed he was the only one who could stop a crisis. Anyway, he was gone the entire evening—supper, games, and all. I usually kept quiet about my disappointment. But that night, Jenna was crushed. So I told Mom off."

"What did she say?" asked Adam.

"Oh, being the Proverbs 31 wife that she is, she stood by her man. *We girls had to share Daddy*, she said. *We should not be greedy because he was helping save the children of Africa.* I remember crying myself to sleep that night wanting to be as important to him as the African children were."

"Everyone wants to save the world," mused Adam.

"Welcome to the fallout ..." Kendra sung to herself, mimicking a line from her favorite song.

DOING FAMILY

Adam and Kendra are fictional characters, but sadly, their account has one of those "Inspired by a True Story" labels slapped on it. All of the parent-child struggles depicted are from the actual experiences of kids I've talked to who grew up in Christian homes. I wish I could say that I was guilty of being melodramatic to drive a point home, focusing on an obscure pair of troubled souls who fell through the cracks, who made the wrong choices in spite of the best efforts of their parents. But the scandal of the modern evangelical family is that young adults like Adam and Kendra are proving to be the rule, not the exception.

Studies consistently show that as Bible-based believing teens head off to college, the vast majority of them leave their Bible at home. A recent Barna Research study found that 60 percent of teens actively involved in spiritual activities will likely not continue in their faith as they become adults. That's six out of ten kids who go to early morning Bible studies, wear the latest Jesus apparel, listen to Christian music on their iPods, and never miss a youth group meeting. The study points out that this is not just a rebellious phase either, but a long-term change that continues into their middle-age years.

A recent UCLA study supports Barna's findings. It found that eight out of ten college freshman said that they attended church services frequently or occasionally during the final years of high school. Yet only three of ten would make the same claim during college. In analyzing these discouraging statistics, Christian commentators are quick to point to the need to overhaul youth ministry and church programming. One Christian journalist remarked that "there must be a brutally honest re-examination of how we do church."

Perhaps a far more worthwhile reexamination is of *how we do family*. The essential hands-on role of the father so easily glides under the radar. The cause-effect relationship of Proverbs 22:6 ("Start children off on the way they should go, and when they are old they will not turn from it") is being overlooked. Christian men are content to act like head coaches, overseeing others raise their kids—teachers at school, youth pastors at church, and Mom at home. The results speak for themselves: the faith of millions of Christian teens is proving to be the seed of the sower that falls on rocky ground—received initially with joy but which has no root and soon withers away (Matt. 13:19).

Being a solo climber is a dangerous business for a man—both on the mountain sides and inside the home. "They're strictly playing Russian roulette," is how mountain guide Lou Whittaker describes solo climbers. "They're walking on stuff with hundreds of holes in it. Every year people drop through. Some live, some die." In the same way, too many sincere, driven, and responsible Christian men today are playing Russian roulette with their families. They believe that if they devote themselves to work and ministry and maintain a Christian household, their church-grown kids are being adequately fed and will stay put at Base Camp, so to speak. Yet, just as on the mountain, the odds are stacked against solo acts—most of these church-grown teens will lose their faith when they become adults.

In recent years, more and more men seem to be coming to terms with their responsibilities. Men's ministries are growing in numbers and motivating men to deal with these home issues head on. After I crashed and burned at work and began my restoration, I looked to these popular evangelical solutions. I too wanted to be that man of integrity in all aspects of my life. I wanted to be a Balanced Man.

THREE STRIKES

Balance was the word I saw sprinkled everywhere when I looked for answers to overcome my career/family struggles. I remember reading an article called "The Right Balance," telling me how to become *both* a career man and a family man. I attended a men's conference challenging attendees to live a balanced life. It seemed like every Christian men's book, magazine, or ministry had the same consistent message—b-a-l-a-n-c-e. This advice had proven elusive to many other Christian men, but I was convinced their failure was simply because they didn't follow the plan.

In balance, I had discovered my new mantra, my salvation. I was righting the ship I had wronged. My family was still intact, and my kids still had many more years at home. John le Carre wrote a novel back in the 1960s entitled *The Spy Who Came in from the Cold*. I felt like I was *The Man Who Came in from the Cold*; I was coming in from the periphery of my family into its center.

I took this Balanced Man attitude with me when I started a new job in Silicon Valley. *My career would never again seduce me and take over my life*, I vowed. I would work reasonable hours and not allow myself to do constant all-nighters just to make a software release date. And, for the first several months into the job, my plan seemed to work. I was around home much more than ever before. We were doing far more together as a family, and no one seemed happier and more content than Kim was.

But as time passed, this balancing act became harder and harder to pull off. Unavoidable demands at the office forced me to work longer hours. *Move one step toward the office.* Promotion opportunities were popping up all over the place, and my career seemed to be on the fast track. *Move three more giant steps.*

In my men's accountability group, I could justify my schedule to my friends, because on paper, my calendar said I was still leading a balanced life. Yet, deep in my heart, I didn't buy it. I felt as if I were being ripped and tugged from all directions. My wife or kids began to feel neglected, so I turned my attention homeward. *Move one step toward home.* Then, when a deadline or cool new project came along, I shifted my energy back toward my career. *Move one step back.* My balancing act turned into an exercise of corrective measures, counter measures, and constant tweaking, trying to find the "sweet spot" that would bring everything into harmony. *Strike one.*

Fast forward four years, and I left that fast company and took a position at a much slower-paced one, with few challenges and opportunities for career growth. I took the role in large part because it seemed like the best situation for my family. *Move four giant steps toward home.* My work-family struggle continued, though ironically it manifested itself in an almost opposite way than before. Instead of struggling to beat down my drive to work, I was struggling with the desire to work at all. I shifted my focus so much toward the home front that I had devolved into the Expectations Guy — so preoccupied with being a responsible father and husband that my lifelong passion and zest for my vocation was dulled and clouded. I hated my job — the very thing my heart was looking to for adventure and purpose. *Strike two.*

For two years, I sought a change from this watered-down life. What I really wanted to do was pursue my dream of writing Christian books full time. I'll jump ahead for the sake of the story, but I eventually received a book opportunity from a publisher. Convinced of God's blessing and timing, I decided to jump in head first.

In leaving my office on the last day of work, I was certain that my new career was the culmination of everything I had been working for and praying about for years. It was the best of both worlds — performing a job that I loved and doing it at home with my family. I was sure that I could finally become the Balanced Man that had always eluded me in three different high-tech jobs. That would prove to be wishful thinking. Within a matter of weeks, the same struggles were resurfacing yet again. I still had deadlines; I was just nearer in proximity to my family as I was working to complete them. I could be with the family at dinner each day, but still be distracted thinking about a chapter I needed to write later that evening. I could be out playing ball with my boys, but still wish I was back in my office getting things done.

In the end, in spite of the fact that I had created the ideal environment in which to thrive as a Balanced Man, I could not pull it off. *Strike three.* For the first time, I began to see the entire concept of a Balanced Man as more than just elusive. It now seemed fatally flawed.

I picked up a copy of an Everest climbing book one evening to veg out, but ended up becoming captivated by the story of elite climber Anatoli Boukreev. The more I learned about Boukreev, the more I felt as if I were looking into one of those wacky carnival mirrors and viewing a distorted version of myself.

THE CARNIVAL MIRROR

Anatoli Boukreev was one of the most accomplished high-altitude solo climbers in the world. Everything in his life reinforced this fact. He was brash, bold, and confident. Maybe it was his Russian background. Russian mountaineering culture has a history of being a tough, self-reliant crowd. Perhaps it was his long list of accomplishments. After all, by the mid-1990s, he'd ascended seven of the world's fourteen highest peaks (including Everest twice)—all without supplemental oxygen. Therefore, when Boukreev was hired by Scott Fischer in 1996 to serve as a supporting guide on his Mountain Madness team, he brought this fiercely independent attitude with him.

Fischer's team was ascending Everest in May of that year on a nearly identical schedule as Rob Hall's Adventure Consultants expedition. You will recall that Rob Hall, Doug Hansen, and several others from the Adventure Consultants expedition lost their lives in their summit attempt. Fischer's team would have results just as disastrous.

While Boukreev had the title of "guide" on the expedition, he functioned much more like a solo climber. During the whole acclimatization process, he was off doing his own thing—hauling loads, marking routes, and preparing the ropes. On summit day, instead of playing the role of caretaker and belaying other team members and guiding them to the top, Boukreev went ahead on his own straight to the top. Then, not waiting for anyone, he proceeded back downward while other team members were still climbing up. By late afternoon, while several members of Fischer's team were fighting for their lives in the midst of a sudden, blinding snowstorm, Boukreev was safely back inside his tent at Camp 4.

Many experienced guides questioned whether Boukreev's actions were appropriate for a guide on summit day. Other observers were even more outspoken, claiming his behavior was pure selfishness—by putting his own accomplishments and interests above the team. Author Jon Krakauer recounts the story of one member of Fischer's team as being particularly outraged, convinced that when it mattered most, Boukreev "cut and ran."

Boukreev, however, had a much different take. He insisted that he was just following orders. According to Boukreev, Scott Fischer asked him to go down to Camp 4 to prepare for others returning and to gather replacement oxygen tanks that could be used for people in trouble. Besides, Boukreev insisted, it was never his job to help other team members en route. "What is guiding Everest?" asked Boukreev. "I don't know what being an Everest guide means. I am a coach, not a guide." He believed Everest was no place for inexperienced climbers who couldn't make it to the top by themselves. In his mind, he was to act like a super Sherpa, making sure supplies were in place rather than helping team members up the mountain.

When I first read about Boukreev, I dismissed him out of hand. After all, Boukreev's attitude, when seen in light of the disaster that occurred, seems selfish, outrageous, or at least terribly misguided. Yet, as I reflected more on his perspective on guiding, I wondered if, underneath the brashness, it was really all that different from the attitude that I—and many other Christian men—have toward fatherhood.

To Boukreev, it simply made no sense for him to change his way of doing things, to sacrifice all of his personal goals in the process of guiding Everest. In his mind, he was convinced that he could do both. Similarly, for many years I was certain that I could have the "right balance"—a career man from nine to five and a family man on nights and weekends—with no cost to my family.

In order to pull off his balancing act, Boukreev changed the definition of a guide: he was a coach, not a caretaker. "I am a coach, a coach to sportsmen," repeated Boukreev. "I offer my expertise and experience for hire in order to help a group of people reach the summit. But am I responsible for whether they live or die? I am not. I will advise them on how to reach the summit, I will show them how, and I will help them, but I cannot be responsible for their safety." In fact, because he didn't believe in coddling climbers, he thought it irresponsible to act any differently.

Similarly, in attempting to live a balanced life, I naturally defined "head of household" and "spiritual leader" in terms that would fit into my career and ministry obligations—as a coach more than a hands-on guide. Biblical fatherhood was providing, overseeing, monitoring, motivating, encouraging, and advising—as if those responsibilities, in and of themselves, were enough. I also didn't take the cause-and-effect relationship of Proverbs 22:6 seriously. Like Boukreev's hands-off attitude toward other climbers, I didn't accept responsibility for my children's long-term spiritual state. *Because they have free will*, I reasoned, *I am not responsible for what choices they will make later in life.*

In the end, Boukreev tried and failed to balance his solo pursuits with his role as guide. So did I. It is just easier to see the mistakes in his decision-making since the results were so immediate and devastating. It takes most men years before they see the results of their fathering decisions.

"There is a way that appears to be right," says Proverbs

14:12. Balance is a solution that seems so practical in theory, that "seems right." Yet it proves itself to be hollow and unbiblical at its core. "We have misplaced common sense," is how Jonah33 sums up the mistakes of today's Christian fathers in "Father's Song." Unless you can clone yourself, it's impossible to be a career man and a family man at the same time. You are either one or the other. When a man tries to do both, he ends up as a lukewarm mishmash, reminiscent of something Christ says he would spit out of his mouth (Rev. 3:16).

At some point, it finally dawned on me why I kept failing at this balancing act. As contradictory as it sounds, I don't think work and family were really the principal actors in this drama. Instead, I was attempting to constantly balance adventure at work with responsibility at home, purpose with duty, and what I longed to do with what I was accountable for. The fallacy of the Balanced Man is that we think we can come up with the right recipe that gives a man a dose of what he is searching for and a dose of what his family needs.

When I was a software developer, I spent a lot of time debugging and stress testing a program I had created. The debugging process was typically iterative. I used the application and, when I encountered a bug, I went back into the code, tweaked it, and tried again. However, once in awhile, I would encounter a crasher bug, one that brought down the whole computer system. At that point, I couldn't do anything on my computer, because no application would respond. The only solution was to hit the giant Reset button on the front of my computer to reboot and rework the code before debugging again.

When I considered the failed attempts in my life at biblical fatherhood—as the Rugged Individualist,

Expectations Guy, and the Balanced Man — it became apparent that each of these models contained "crasher bugs," so to speak. They each showed the propensity to bring down my life when they were stress tested. A reboot was necessary. Everything was thus set for the "system restart" that would soon rock my world and forever change the way I looked at my career and family.

PART 2

MAPPING THE ASCENT

The work of the guide implies abnegation. The guide does not go where he wants to go, but must go to the summit of which his client has dreamed. The guide does not climb for himself but primarily for the pleasure of the companion he is leading.
—Gaston Rebuffat

An adventure is only an inconvenience rightly considered. An inconvenience is only an adventure wrongly considered.
—G. K. Chesterton

CHAPTER 4

FROM SOLO CLIMBER TO TEAM LEADER

A climb has a beginning, a middle, and an end. It has a clear purpose — getting to the summit and dealing with the intricacies of the route and the sense of exposure — and it has a clear outcome — you reach the summit or you do not. It is not vague or uncertain or equivocal, like so much of modern life ... Nothing epitomizes the idea of accomplishment and satisfaction one gets from it better than climbing to the top of the mountain.
— Jochen Hemmleb

I call it The Metamorphosis. And I still don't know when exactly it occurred. Maybe the change happened as I heard Jared praying from the heart one particular evening or watching Justy lead our family Bible study. Or perhaps the trigger was witnessing Jordan apply his faith to the issue he was debating in history class. More likely, it happened when I got off by myself and spent time alone with God. I didn't exactly realize it at the time, but God was gradually changing my way of thinking about work and family, adventure and responsibility.

I had been working at home as an author for several months. At the start, the changes for me were just geographical (working down the hall instead of down the highway) and vocational (authoring Christian books, not developing software). My drive was clearly for my writing —

something I'd passionately wanted to do as a profession for years. But as time passed, God began to work on my spirit. The dictionary defines *metamorphosis* as the process of dramatically changing from one form to another. I can't think of a word that better describes what was going on inside me at that time. I emerged as more of a presence and influence in the household than I had ever been before. I spent more time just being with my family, more involved with schooling the boys, and more intent in looking for discipling opportunities. Most significantly, however, my ideas of purpose and adventure—things I've been consumed with my entire life—were being leveled and rebuilt.

My adventure was no longer just my career; it was *everything* I was doing at 22 Lyon Road. The puzzle pieces of my career, family, and ministry were actually fitting together rather than overlapping. This shift was not just a straw-man's dream. I wasn't dousing my dreams and desires with duty. I wasn't force-fitting adventure onto my family like a *Spy Kids* movie. And while I was aware something major was happening, it took a mountain half a world away to help me really understand what was going on inside me.

I am a big believer in the power of metaphor. God has designed the human race to grasp spiritual truths through storytelling at a level deeper than we can with principles alone. Metaphor has the "mysterious ability to capture much more about reality than monotone literalness could ever dream," writes Douglas Jones. While literal speech is one dimensional, metaphor "shoots off in many directions at once." During his earthly ministry, Jesus Christ certainly understood the power of metaphor in reaching the hearts and minds of his followers. He chose to deliver his teaching through parables, not thirty-minute theological exhortations from the pulpit.*

Metaphor has certainly helped shape my faith. I have learned more about the amazing nature of grace reading *Les Misérables* and watching the film *Babette's Feast* than I have from any hefty scholarly book on the subject. I have discovered more about honor and virtue watching *Braveheart* and *Rob Roy* than doing a word study on them. Or consider my good friend Philip. He read every one of C. S. Lewis's apologetic books and came to my weekly Bible study, but it wasn't until he saw Mel Gibson's *The Passion of the Christ* that Christianity became real to him and he became a believer.

That's why the whole topic of fatherhood suffers in comparison: the subject is treated so utterly practically and factually in Christian circles. It's dull. I'll go to a men's conference and hear about "six steps to becoming a biblical father." Or, in a Christian men's magazine, I'll turn to a cut-out accountability checklist for keeping career and family in balance. Frankly, fatherhood has never been a subject matter that has inspired rich metaphor and allegory.

The danger of practical teaching alone is that it often comes wrapped in a Teflon coating. I remember getting

---

* New Testament scholar Kenneth Bailey says that Christ used parables to teach because metaphor has a higher potential for meaning. In our Western thinking, we believe that concepts are the most important ideas, while metaphors are considered secondary. Illustrations are commonly used only to simplify a concept or are employed as a tool to help us remember. Yet, from a Middle Eastern perspective, a parable or metaphor actually *creates* meaning in a way that goes above and beyond the concept. Therefore, according to Bailey, metaphors reach us on a deeper level—they speak to the whole person in a way that concepts or principles alone do not. See Kenneth Bailey, *Finding the Lost: Cultural Keys to Luke 15* (St. Louis: Concordia Scholarship Today, 1992).

pumped up annually at a Promise Keeper's event or a weekend men's retreat, only to fall back just three or four weeks later into the same ruts I had struggled with before. If the teaching a man hears doesn't penetrate and cling to his spirit, then lasting change is a tough haul.

Men are practical creatures; we are doers, task driven. But that doesn't mean that we grow by reading only concepts and principles. We also want to be inspired. We need to grab hold of something larger than ourselves. Why else are films like *Braveheart* and *Gladiator* so adored by men? Why else does a men's book like *Wild at Heart* sell millions?

I have long been drawn to Mount Everest. I am not sure if my attraction is the awesome geography, the life-or-death nature of the environs, or the exploits of the climbers that have scaled it. The British poet William Blake once wrote, "Great things are done when men and mountains meet; / This is not done by jostling in the street." Blake's poetic lyric gets to the heart of my attraction—I see greatness, risk, and reward happening on Everest, something far more difficult to see here at 834 feet above sea level. Everest climbing historian Jochen Hemmleb adds, "Your senses are completely alert when you're climbing—hearing, breathing, smelling, everything—and you begin to get a glimpse of how deep the feeling of being alive can really become." Thus, when I found myself seeking greatness, purpose, and "the feeling of being alive" in my life, I was struck by the parallels I saw between the leaders of these expeditions and the newfound adventures I was experiencing at home. I began to see that, more than anything else I've come across, an Everest expedition provides a modern-day parable for biblical manhood. Everest provided that rich metaphor that I had been searching for.

A NEW ROLE

A modern Everest mountaineering expedition is composed of a team of climbers, hired Sherpas to help with supplies, and a team leader. Climbers come from all walks of life. Some are experienced, others far less. The expedition leader will usually hire a couple of expert climbers to come along to help guide. The expedition goal is straightforward — to climb to the top of the mountain and live to tell about it.

The great challenge is, of course, actually pulling it off. Over the past fifty years, experience has shown that successful expeditions have always had a common ingredient to them — strong, hands-on leadership. They have had a leader who encourages, protects, and instructs his team; who understands the limitations of each climber and plans accordingly; and who manages egos to create and preserve a unity and common bond. When I look at the role of the expeditionary guide, I compare him to a servant leader, a "shepherd" of his team. He has several responsibilities that parallel the role of a biblical father. Let me explain.

Directs the path. The leader of an Everest expedition collaborates with guides and Sherpas on his team, but he is ultimately responsible and accountable for driving the route and summit schedule. In the same way, a man is charged with being responsible for the goals, directions, and decisions of his family (1 Cor. 11:3). While he is leader, he obviously works hand in hand with his wife as they raise their children and maintain the household. But following the biblical model laid out by Paul, a man should serve his wife and family as Christ does the church (Eph. 5:25).

Trains and instructs. An expeditionary leader trains and instructs his team. The members of commercial expeditions do not have the needed skills, expertise, or experience to climb the mountain on their own. The leader (and his hired guides for larger teams) provides constant, up-close training during the acclimatization process. A guide knows that the lives of the individuals he is caring for depend on his success in preparing and equipping them for the task.

Likewise, the Scriptures consistently portray a father as being hands-on, proactive in instruction. Paul exhorts the fathers in Ephesus to "bring [their children] up in the training and instruction of the Lord" (Eph. 6:4). He is not free to simply delegate this responsibility to the youth pastor, to the church, or even to the kids themselves. A passage in Deuteronomy 6 is even more sweeping in nature. Consider all of the active verbs being used (emphasis mine): "These commandments that I give you today are to be on your hearts. *Impress* them on your children. *Talk* about them when you sit at home and when you walk along the road, when you lie down and when you get up. *Tie* them as symbols on your hands and *bind* them on your foreheads. *Write* them on the doorframes of your houses and on your gates" (Deut. 6:6–9). The language Moses uses here is frenetic, sounding almost ADHD in intensity — *first do this, then this, then this, and then this.* Clearly, discipling and teaching children is, according the Scriptures, a constant, ongoing activity. This depiction of biblical fatherhood stands in stark contrast to the stereotype of the out-of-touch father who comes home from work too exhausted to involve himself with his family.

Engineers unity. As he equips and serves the team, an expeditionary leader actively works to build unity amongst the team members. Given the headstrong personalities often attracted to mountain climbing, this is no easy task. Through constant efforts, he builds an environment of trust and cohesion. He teaches them to belay, or attach a fixed rope to another climber to protect each other against a fall. By the time the team approaches the extreme altitudes of Everest, they must be able to work together, depend on each other, and trust one another with their lives—knowing that there's another person on the end of the 150-foot rope who is willing to risk life and limb for them. Jon Krakauer puts it like this, "Roping up in this fashion is a serious and very intimate act." Jochen Hemmleb adds, "When you know you have to rely on another person for your own safety, and he upon you, you learn a level of trust that simply doesn't exist very often in the normal world."

An expedition team's ability to trust and count on each other high on the mountain is often the difference between life and death. The story of American mountaineer Pete Schoening is perhaps the best demonstration of this truth. In 1953, Pete was on an eight-man American expedition team to climb K2, the second largest mountain in the world at 28,250 feet. On the way, they got stuck at around 25,000 feet when a massive ten-day blizzard pounded the mountain. While they were held up, team member Art Gilkey developed thrombophlebitis, a life-threatening blood clot caused by the high altitude. The condition left Art unable to walk. The rest of the team knew that Art would die if he did not descend immediately. Rather than split into two groups, they decided that they would descend together or not at all. "It was a job that needed to get done," said expedition leader Charles Houston. "We had to get Art off that mountain."

The team began to lower Art, who was now wrapped in a sleeping bag, down a steep ridge in the middle of the snowstorm. Suddenly, one of the climbers slipped on a sixty-degree slope, causing a chain reaction that pulled four others who were roped together off the mountain. In a split-second action, Schoening wrapped the rope around himself, jammed his ice axe into a rock, and miraculously held on for dear life. In this incredible feat of heroism, Schoening arrested the fall of the five climbers and held onto Art at the same time. Probably no family will ever face the extreme peril that Schoening and his team did. But a man must be able to create an environment that has this same sense of "die to self" unity that was second nature to Schoening.

Most men are content to simply break up fights, not manufacture unity at home. I live in a house with three boys, and I can tell you with authority that family unity is an engineered peace; it doesn't come naturally. Petty squabbles, ongoing disagreements, and hardened attitudes will form unless a man is relentless in stomping these attitudes out—but without stomping on his family in the process (Eph. 6:4). A man must avoid accepting sibling rivalries, biting sarcasm, and sinful behaviors that are accepted and joked about by the world. He needs to work hard to provide an environment that encourages friendship and loyalty among his kids.

That's why spending a lot of time together as a family is such a critical decision a man needs to make. One of the nasty side effects of a family going in separate directions all week is that they will invariably find it impossible to pull together in the rare moments that they are under one roof. However, the more families work, play, and study alongside each other on a day-to-day basis, the more family members develop an uncommon bond that is rarely seen in today's postmodern world.

Thinks long term. The expedition leader is always planning to ensure the well-being of his entire team, even when his decision goes against their will. "Going up is optional, getting down is mandatory" is the motto of expert climber Ed Viesturs. More than once while serving as guide, Ed has turned around within site of the summit. Ed explains, "As we were going up, I was already processing going down. That's my training as a guide: to think, This is happening now — what are the consequences for later?" Sometimes the guide has to have the foresight and tenacity to turn around, even when that decision is unpopular. Expedition leader Rob Hall's decision making on Everest with Doug Hansen in 1996 shows the tragic consequences when the guide loses perspective and fails to look out for the long-term interests of a team member.

Similarly, biblical fatherhood requires a man to ensure that the activities his family is involved with are consistent with the goal of producing disciples and strengthening family relationships. Tough decisions may need to be made, even if that means stopping his family in their tracks. *Is it wise for my kids to be in soccer this year if it constantly scatters our family in three directions? Should I drop out of the Tuesday night men's Bible study since it is on the one free night of the week for our family?* Think ahead and identify the consequences, and then have the fortitude to "turn around" everyone else when that call is needed.

Sacrifices personal ambition. As an expert climber, a team leader loves nothing more than to take on new challenges on a summit attempt. After all, few people get more than a handful of cracks at Everest in their lifetime. From a personal standpoint, he would prefer to take tougher routes than the popular South Col route to the summit. But he knows that the northern routes are too technically difficult for a normal team to make. Even more, he would like to climb without supplemental oxygen—since an un-aided climb is highly preferred among the mountaineer-ing purists. But he declines, since guiding without oxygen bottles is considered reckless by most guides.

As you can see, an Everest expeditionary leader needs to be willing to sacrifice personal ambition in one of the most ambitious places on earth. The famous French alpinist Gaston Rebuffat reflects on the sacrificial role of the guide:

> The work of the guide implies abnegation. The guide does not go where he wants to go, but must go to the summit of which his client has dreamed. The guide does not climb for himself but primarily for the plea-sure of the companion he is leading.

The sacrifice the expedition leader makes is a remarkable picture of a biblical father—a man who puts his personal goals on hold while his kids are in the home, since so many of those ambitions are not compatible with the spiritual and emotional well-being of his family.

Not that such sacrifice is easy. Remember the scene in *Field of Dreams* in which Shoeless Joe asks writer Terence Mann to come with the ballplayers into the cornfield to see what lies "beyond." Ray Kinsella, the man who built the ball field, is frustrated. In a flash of selfishness, Ray asks Shoeless Joe why he is not invited to come, particu-larly because he sees himself as the reason for all of this happening in the first place. Listen to their interchange:

RAY KINSELLA: I did it all. I listened to the voices, I did what they told me, and not once did I ask what's in it for me.

SHOELESS JOE: What are you saying, Ray?
RAY KINSELLA: I'm saying ... what's in it for me?
SHOELESS JOE: Is that why you did this? For you?

Just like Ray, a man can get sidetracked and start look-ing at how devoted he is, deluding himself into believing he deserves more for all of his dedication and sacrifice. Yet, the lesson of the film is that, had Ray remained self-ishly bent on getting his way, he would have missed the real blessing intended for him at the end of the story. Likewise, when a man sacrifices his own personal ambi-tion, the blessing from his new role is often something far more fulfilling than what he would have even dreamt to ask for himself.

Experiences a different adventure. When a solo climber reaches the summit, he gets the Sinatra thrill of saying *I did it my way!* An expeditionary leader will not get the same sense of personal accomplishment when guiding his team up the same trail he's done many times before. But he is rewarded in a completely different way. Guide Dave Hahn understands this well:

> Well, the truth is, guiding is more difficult than climbing. And I like that. I guess I like the combina-tion and the variety that comes with it, but I do enjoy the challenge of guiding, of trying to help somebody safely reach a lifelong goal that might be out of reach if they were left to their own devices.

In the same way, though a man sacrifices personal goals in his career and outside activities, there is another adventure inside the home that is far more thrilling than any job promotion, salary increase, or industry acclaim. It's a family adventure — and it is the heart of what being an Expeditionary Man is all about.

Before I continue, let me clear up a couple of misconceptions that could arise when I speak of a "family adventure." First of all, I am not talking about a man merely dragging his family along for the ride on his own personal crusades. Those Chevy Chase *Vacation* films from the 1980s immediately come to mind: an overly excited dad gets a reluctant wife and whiny kids to go on a family adventure across the country. Shared family activities are a part of a "family adventure," but they are not the primary focus.

Second, a man's adventure is not his family in and of itself. "Family man" is a nice label to have, but it's not the be-all, end-all goal that most men have in life. We're simply not wired that way. A man can try this for a while, but he will grow restless and begin looking for outlets for his pent-up energy and creativity.

I have to stress that I am not trying to pull a bait and switch—passing off responsibility as adventure. To stress the practical reality of what I am talking about, let me move away from the mountains for a moment and turn to a more familiar world for many of you. Let me talk about Sam, a CEO that I used to work under. The way in which he performed his job offers a compelling model for how a man can lead his family.

A New Adventure

Sam was the CEO of a young startup company I worked for several years ago. When the company launched, the flagship product was in a hotly competitive market with several big-time players. Sam knew that going head-to-head against the likes of Microsoft and Adobe would be tough, but he thrived on the adversity. His job early on was to build a strong core team and make sure everyone in the company was working toward the same objective—delivering the best website-building software to the marketplace.

Sam previously worked as a senior director of R&D at Apple and loved the challenge of developing software and designing a product's internal architecture. However, in his new leadership role, Sam knew he had to adjust. He could not allow himself to get distracted by what he selfishly would love to do—be intimately involved in the overall design of the product. If he did so, he would end up sacrificing his time on tactical issues rather than the company's long-term strategic objectives.

Sam regularly spent time with different parts of the company. For example, he sometimes joined the sales team on an important sales call or dropped in on the support department when a major customer was having problems. Such activities, no matter how mundane they may have been, were helping the company meet its big-picture goals.

When I consider the role that Sam played at the company, I see "Expeditionary Man" written all over it. A man should think of his role in his home much like that of a hands-on CEO of his household. He leads by serving. He's in charge, but not aloof. He partners closely with his wife to form a unified leadership team. He's actively engaged with his children, but always in authority. He loves what he does for a profession, but never gets distracted from the big-picture goals of the family.

When a man lives out this hands-on leadership role, his idea of adventure and purpose will inevitably change. He will become so preoccupied with leading his family that his old passions and desires for adventure in things outside the home begin to take a backseat.

Expert guides will tell you that guiding an expedition is much different from climbing it. As a result, they often struggle in making the transition. Climbing expert Lou Whittaker says, "There are many good climbers, but very few good climbing guides." In the same way, there are many good Christian men providing for their families, but few good hands-on leaders.

Men in the corporate world experience the same difficulty during a job promotion. I know many highly talented individual contributors who have struggled once they became managers. Change is hard, and it is easy for any man to cling to what he knows best.

Bringing this discussion back home, a man needs to embrace this new role and new adventure. Or, to use business book lingo, he needs to "promote himself." He needs to allow himself to step up to his new leadership role in the family and move in from the background.

A New Summit

Once a man begins to assume this leadership role, he is ready to lead his family together toward a new summit—a common destination that each family member can work toward. The summit is not an actual mountaintop, of course, but a goal of who they want *to be* in Christ and what they want *to do* together as a team. When a man carries out this two-pronged "being-doing" strategy, his family will gradually be transformed into, to use a C. S. Lewis term, "little Christs."

John Ruskin once said, "All books are divisible into two classes; the books of the hour and the books of all time." I love Ruskin's dichotomy, and I think we can take it and apply it to the realities of family life by dividing our experiences into two classes: experiences of the hour and experiences of all time.

In living out the life of an Expeditionary Man, a man creates an environment at home that fosters "experiences of all time" as he draws his family together and gets them focused on this common goal and purpose. I can't prove it from Scripture, but I firmly believe that the "unforgettable moments" that a family undertakes are investments—special times that they will joyfully recall and hold as precious throughout eternity.

Let me come back to earth for a minute. One of the slap-in-face realities of living in a society where people go their separate ways for much of the week is that the idea of a family working as a "team" seems out of touch, naïve. A scene from the television series *House, M.D.* makes my point. In the scene, a doctor is asking a series of questions to the father of a deathly ill son in an attempt to diagnose the problem. When the father is unable to answer several of the personal questions being asked, he says, "I guess I don't know what's going on in his life." The doctor shrugs and replies, "He's a teenager," to which the father nods in agreement. From a societal view, this split between a father and teenager is completely expected.

When a man has teenagers living at home, it is often a major challenge simply to get them to talk to him, let alone try to get them on board as team players and interested in doing more together as a family. Take Mike, a man who would like to bring his family together but does not know where to start. While he goes to the office during the day, his wife works several evenings a week. He has a boy and a girl several years apart, both of whom go to separate schools, do their own extracurricular activities, and spend little time together when they are at home. They manage to stay affiliated with each other, but Mike scoffs at the idea of getting his family to even *want* to become a team climbing toward a common summit. "They've each got their own lives," said Mike. "The last thing that they want to do is a bunch of family stuff together. Heck, we're lucky if we can eat together a couple times a week."

On the one hand, Mike is smart not trying to ramrod his vision on a reluctant family and force them into doing something they do not want to do. Such authoritative action would backfire—only breeding contempt and disunity. On the other hand, as the family leader, he cannot simply throw up his hands in surrender. Their reluctance is only the starting point. Since everyone in Mike's family has a different peak they want to climb, his first task is to invest his time and energies into assembling a real team before trying to climb a common mountain together. In the end, Mike needs to see himself as the principal catalyst or change agent that God is calling to make it happen.

A SCREECHING HALT

I once had a chance to direct an engineering team in a research project code-named "Twister." Those of us involved with Twister were convinced that it was going to be the Next Big Thing, blowing away our competition's product offerings. The team worked for several months to make a proof-of-concept prototype that was innovative and showed real promise. But, as impressive as it may have been, the executive leadership did not believe the company had enough resources to make the prototype into a successful product. Ultimately, as hard as it was for my team to stomach, we were forced to leave Twister behind and look for a more fundable Next Big Thing.

Every man who decides to live as an Expeditionary Man will have a new role to play, a new adventure to pursue, and a new summit to climb. But what happens if the pursuit of these callings causes him to risk his ability to provide for his family? As my Twister experience shows, the danger of grandiose ideas and dreams is that, without adequate resources, they always come to a screeching halt. Perhaps that is why my friend Tim is so reluctant to even try.

CHAPTER 5

Beyond the Sherpa

You stay with the group to prevent a disaster;
you don't leave the group to prepare for a disaster.
—Ed Viesturs, climbing expert

"Rich, I would love to be more hands-on with my family," Tim said. "But let's get practical. I have mouths to feed, a house to pay for, and three kids to get through college. You just aren't being realistic." Tim was debating with me the feasibility of the average man, like himself, putting his career on hold for the sake of his family. Tim started his own small company several years ago, but the road to profitability had been tough. As a result, Tim now routinely works at least sixty hours a week just to keep the lights on. He lives under the real fear of business failure and the constant burden of not being able to make enough for his family.

Tim is not alone. Randy thought he had his life mapped out. He had been working at the same company for fifteen years, but now finds himself a victim of corporate downsizing. As much as he would like to give more attention to his family, his overriding concern is finding the best job that provides for his wife and four children. Or consider the plight of my friend Chuck. He works as a middle-level manager in a job he does not like. But in spite of his dissatisfaction, he seems almost incapable of making a change that would put his role as provider at risk.

Every man feels the need, and often an intense pressure, to provide for his family. In fact, when asked what makes a good husband and father, most Christian men will respond that the number one responsibility is to be the breadwinner. As I look around the church, I see evidence of this belief everywhere. A well-known evangelical pastor and author even defines the relationship a man should have with his family in terms of being the provider:

> Men, we are the providers, we are the protectors, we are the preservers, we are the resources for our wives and our families and that is our responsibility. And when their needs are met, and we care for them as we would care for ourselves, then we have the kind of relationship that God wants us to have.

The breadwinner role is viewed as being the most important way in which a man can meet the needs of his family. In his best-selling marriage book, *His Needs, Her Needs*, Willard Harley lists five top needs that a wife has for her husband. Harley goes so far as to place financial support *above* a man's commitment to his family (#4 and #5, respectively). He discusses the type of man who meets this need of his wife:

> He assumes the responsibility to house, feed, and clothe the family. If his income is insufficient to provide essential support, he resolves the problem by upgrading his skills to increase his salary. He does

not work long hours, keeping himself from his wife and family, but is able to provide necessary support by working a 40 to 45 hour work week. While he encourages his wife to pursue a career, he does not depend on her salary for family living expense.

Other studies within the church seem to back up what Harley claims. When Christian women talk about what is most important in a husband, "being a provider" is at or close to the top of the list. Blogger Dan Edelen writes, "You can't read a blog by Christian women and not stumble upon the criteria they use to judge a man to be a proper Christian husband, the first being — always — that he be a good provider."

By and large, the church today sees the biblical model of a family summed up by the following sentiment: *a man provides; a woman runs the household.* People often point to two key passages for defining the roles of the family. A man should observe 1 Timothy 5:8: "Anyone who does not provide for their relatives, and especially for their own household, has denied the faith and is worse than an unbeliever." Meanwhile, a woman should live up to the ideals of Proverbs 31: "She watches over the affairs of her household ..." (31:27). I recently stumbled across a discussion on the Web that captures this perspective:

> Men should be out there doing whatever it takes to insure that mom can spend as much time as possible with her family because she is uniquely equipped by God for the role of managing the household and the kids on a daily basis ... She's better at it than her husband!

As strong of a statement as that is, I don't think men really have much of a problem with this Provider Dad mentality. When I talk with other Christian men about their responsibilities and duties, they never bemoan or argue against it. In fact, they seem to accept—and often rather like—the idea of being the breadwinner as their top priority. The Rugged Individualist, Expectations Guy, and Balanced Man will have different motivations, but each tend to embrace the idea that providing for his family is his number one concern as a husband and father.

For one, the provider role is a responsibility that is tailor-made for a man's no-nonsense personality. Success or failure is easy to gauge: he either is or is not making enough money. If he is not, then his problem-solving skills instinctively kick in to come up with a solution. In contrast, the success of other responsibilities of a Christian man are far trickier to measure. For example, when a man disciples his children and works to strengthen family relationships, the results of his efforts are far less immediate and sometimes impossible to gauge.

Being a Provider Dad is also convenient for a man bent on pursuing adventure in his vocation. It allows us to maximize our career aspirations—all the while justifying ourselves with the *NIV Study Bible* on our desktop. Take Jack as an example. He believes that as long as he spends more than half of his evenings at home and travels just a few days a month, he is perfectly free to climb the corporate ladder. Jack's reasoning is simple: if a man's chief concern is to provide for his family, then he better pursue his career to the utmost.

Many men see taking care of the family's material needs as their "love language," their way of showing the family that they love them. This attitude was engrained in men from earlier generations and is still prevalent today. You see this portrayed in the movie *A Walk in the Clouds*, in an exchange between a stern, emotionally detached father, named Alberto, and Paul, a young man who is in love with Alberto's daughter:

> PAUL: What's your reason ... for shutting your daughter out of your heart? My whole life I've been dreaming of getting the kind of love your daughter tries to give you. I'd die for what you have. Why can't you just love her?

> ALBERTO: You see this? This land? This vineyard? This is 365 days a year. Who do you think I do this for? For them. All of them. I love my family!

To Alberto, Paul's question is insulting. The love he has for his family is self-evident from his standpoint. The sacrifice and dedication he gives to making his vineyard successful is living proof.

A man's responsibility to provide for the physical needs of his family is understood by most believers as being grounded in Scripture. Many point to Adam's curse to work the land in Genesis 3 as God's mandate for a man's role in the family. The Old Testament gives us a window into the patriarchical society and culture of ancient Israel in which a man was responsible to grow and sell crops for his family's material needs. Later, in the New Testament, Paul comes down hard on men who are failing to provide for their households (see 1 Tim. 5:8, above). His statement that a believer who does not provide for his family is even worse than an unbeliever sounds harsh, but he is simply driving at the fact that even pagans in the Roman world understood the basic human responsibility of helping out loved ones.

Clearly, the idea of a man taking responsibility for his family's physical needs is biblical, honorable, and loving. But I am convinced that it is also overglorified by the church today. The far more pressing issue is the tendency of fathers to pay so much attention to material needs that they overlook a family's spiritual needs. As we focus on 1 Timothy 5:8 and 2 Thessalonians 3:10 ("Anyone who is unwilling to work should not eat"), we can overlook the essential teaching found in Deuteronomy 6:6–9 and Ephesians 6:4 ("Fathers ... bring [your children] up in the training and instruction of the Lord"). In fact, the constant pressure a man faces to provide for his family is undoubtedly the single greatest barrier to becoming an Expeditionary Man. Like my friend Tim, he feels as if he has no other choice but to play by the rules of our economy. No other option seems worth the risk.

To be honest, I am starting to believe that popular culture has a better handle on the crucial importance of fathering than do most of us in the church. One of my favorite television shows is *Lost*. On the series, all the main characters have "daddy issues" from their past and are dealing with baggage in the present because of it. Kate had an abusive step-dad and ended up blowing up her house—with her father in it. Sawyer's dad killed his mom and then turned the gun on himself. Jack never felt good enough for his dad and finds himself constantly seeking his approval. And then there is John Locke. His dad swindled John out of a kidney and later threw him out of an eighth-story window. The storylines are obviously far-fetched, but there is something revealing about them. These fictional fathers had many, many problems, but the inability to provide for their families was the least of their "daddy issues."

The tragedy is that most Christian men are far more concerned about saving up to send their children to college than discipling them when they are living under the same roof. Jesus tells us in Mark 8:36, "What good is it for you to gain the whole world, yet forfeit your soul?" Perhaps we should come up with a New Father's Translation of the Bible that paraphrases that verse something like this: "What does it profit a man if he can afford a big house and an Ivy League education for his kids, only to have them fall away from their faith when they get to Harvard?"

ART OF THE FATHER

On every Everest expedition, adequate supplies are an essential part of a trip's success. From the roads, the provisions are carried over twenty miles by porters and yaks across the lower hills and valleys to Base Camp. But once the real climbing begins above Base Camp at 22,000 feet, the four higher camps must be stocked by the team climbing up. Food, water, shelter, technical equipment, and multiple bottles of oxygen are required for each team member. In all, more than 2,500 items are needed just to get one climber to the top. Clearly, without reliable and effective assistance in supplying these camps, there could be no summit bid for the team.

Ever since the earliest expeditions up Everest in the 1920s, Western climbers have employed locally available Sherpas to carry supplies. Sherpas are an ethnic group of people in Nepal populating the surrounding regions. Living at high altitudes, Sherpas have adapted physiologically to deal with the smaller amounts of oxygen in the air. Not surprisingly, they have proven themselves as "naturals" for hauling supplies to the expedition camps high up the mountain. Working under the leadership and direction of the expedition leader, a small group of Sherpas are contracted to make sure that the camps are well stocked, ladders are placed across crevasses, and ropes are properly laid at strategic points on the route.

Imagine, for a moment, a different scenario. Suppose an expeditionary team arrives at Everest and, for whatever reason, is unable to hire any Sherpas. The leader knows that the team, which is made up of first-time Everesters, stands no chance of being able to take their own supplies up the mountain. But instead of canceling the trip, the leader decides that he will do the work of the Sherpa himself. He convinces himself he can balance the leader and provider roles. As the weeks go by during the acclimatization process, however, he ends up spending all day carrying the supplies up the mountain to stock the camps. Only a cursory amount of time is spent training and instructing the team members. He just does not have the energy for it. So when the expedition team is finally in a position to try for the summit, they are a disaster waiting to happen, the mountaineering version of the Bad News Bears. The leader may have been successful providing for the team's material needs, but he has left a leadership vacuum in the process. In the end, the well-supplied but ill-prepared team stands little chance of success.

You can probably see by now where I am going with this story. The role of the Sherpa on an Everest expedition is remarkably similar to the Provider Dad mentality. The primary job for both of them is to meet the material needs of the people he is responsible for. Feed. Clothe. Provide shelter. That sort of thing. Many Christian men play the role of Sherpa to a "T." They take pride in working hard so their families do not have to. They receive satisfaction knowing that they have taken care of the physical needs of their family. They've been doing it so long their bodies have adapted to it, so to speak. The problem is, however, that a man is never called to be just a Sherpa to his family. He's also called to lead and to guide.

If a man's number-one priority is to be Provider Dad, then he will never be able to effectively lead his family. Not only does he undervalue their spiritual needs, but he overvalues material needs in the eyes of his children. As a result, he will produce kids far more interested in what is inside of the supply tent than what is on top of the mountain.

Wait a minute, Rich, you may be saying. *On Everest, an expedition leader delegates that responsibility to the Sherpas he hires. But a man simply cannot hand off that responsibility. A dad has to serve as both leader and provider, right?* True, and I certainly deal with that underlying tension every day. I must provide for my family, but I can't shirk back from my leadership role in the process. I don't have all the answers on how to manage the two responsibilities, but there is one thing I do know for certain: no matter how important the provider role is, it is *always* secondary to the leader role. If you prefer, you can think of the two responsibilities as being one-A and one-B in terms of priority, as long as family leadership always occupies that one-A slot. Let me explain.

Providing is short-term, leading is long-term. Being a provider is the most short-term and temporal of all the responsibilities of a man. Nothing he does in this role lasts for long. To be honest, if I were an unbeliever, I am not sure I'd feel the same way. After all, if this world is all there is, then it seems far more reasonable to be more concerned about the financial security of your family than almost anything else. *Be safe, secure, and comfortable for as long as possible* goes the worldview. But Jesus Christ calls us to a different mindset. He tells believers to be "in the world but not of the world" (see John 17:15–16, 18) because he has something far more lasting in eternity. In other words, when push comes to shove, the spiritual lives of a man's family matter more.

Providing is tactical, leading is strategic. The words *strategy* and *tactics* are often used interchangeably. However, from a military perspective, their meanings are distinct from each other. Derived from the Greek *strategos* (meaning "general"), *strategy* refers to the overall big-picture planning of a military campaign. In other words, it's the "art of the general." Think D-Day invasion or the Allied march to Berlin ... the big stuff. In contrast, tactics deal with the execution of plans on a smaller scale—Easy Company taking out the cannons of a German battery or raiding the town of Carentan—that sort of thing.

When a man disciples and leads his family, he is focused on responsibilities of strategic importance—you could call it the "art of the father." The breadwinner role, by contrast, is pure tactics. Making money is significant only as it enables more important strategies of biblical leadership to be carried out in the home.

By all accounts, the apostle Paul never had a wife or children. Nonetheless, he gives us a biblical model for understanding how to manage the strategic and provider responsibilities of a man's life. According to Acts 18:3, Paul generated income for himself by being a tentmaker. However, as you read his letters, you get the sense that tentmaking was a practical matter for the apostle. He may have enjoyed the job, but he did it to support his real calling—his ministry to the Gentiles. In fact, I suspect that when people talked with Paul, his trade rarely came up (except perhaps when trying to engage other tentmakers). Likewise, a man can love his job and receive immense satisfaction from it, but it should not distract him from what is far more important.

Providing separates, while leading unifies. The relationship of a Provider Dad to his family has some loose parallels to the interpersonal relationship of a Sherpa to the expeditionary team. As the Sherpa performs his duties, he spends his day apart from the rest of the climbers. It's not surprising, then, that a Sherpa tends to be on the outside of the team, not part of the inner circle. Similarly, the Provider Dad is often gradually pulled away as the demands of work take their toll on his relationship with his family. This separation is almost imperceptible at the start. But as time goes on, the lack of intimacy will reach the point where his family consciously or unconsciously writes him off. In the end, the Provider Dad becomes the Peripheral Dad.

In contrast, a leadership role draws a man inward toward his family at an exponential rate—the longer a man invests in his family, the greater the magnitude of the return. The initial years are often a necessary investment in relationship building that pays off in a big way as time goes on.

CATCH–22

How does a man fulfill his responsibility to provide for his family without it distracting him from his leadership role? It's a classic catch–22: a man needs to provide for his family in order to have a household to lead, but his work commitments prevent him from being an effective leader at home.

Consider this quandary in the context of the hypothetical, do-it-all expeditionary leader referred to in the previous section. He opted to concentrate on the Sherpa role because the consequences of not providing seemed clear-cut—his team would not have adequate supplies to make it up the mountain. By contrast, the actual costs of neglecting the team were far less certain to him. He could rationalize to himself, *Well, they might be okay*, overlooking the obvious dangers of taking an inexperienced and ill-prepared team to the top of Everest.

But suppose there were legitimate alternatives to the zero-sum game he was playing. He could have divided up the Sherpa responsibilities with stronger members of the team, eliminated all but the bare essential supplies, trained the team at the start of the day, and then loaded supplies up the mountain afterward, or even creatively trained the team while hauling supplies. None of these would be ideal solutions, but they were workable options he could have chosen.

Bringing this back to real life, the ideal is for a man to provide fully for his family all the while assuming a hands-on leadership role in his home. He is able to organize his schedule so that he can both work and be a consistent, engaged presence with his family. However, that idyllic model is not always possible. After all, a dual-income family is a practical reality for millions of couples today as more and more men are sharing the provider role with their wives.

In my case, Kim and I were convinced that, though she had been a stay-at-home mom for over a decade, she should go back to work as a nurse on a part-time basis to help make up the difference in income that existed after I left my high-tech job. The decision was tough on both of us. Kim loved being at home focused on the boys, and I felt saddened, even a bit ashamed, at taking her away from that—even if only a few days a week. But we pushed ahead anyway, convinced that her return to nursing was for a reason (opening up the chance for me to serve God in this manner) and for a season (once I got further established, we believed the need for her to work would lessen).

A smaller number of men go so far as to hand over the entire responsibility to their wives as they stay at home with the kids. However, except for brief seasons of a man's life, I wonder about the wisdom of this move. My reasoning is less biblical than practical—frankly, I don't believe a stay-at-home dad role really works for most men over the long run. They won't find lasting fulfillment playing "Mr. Mom." Rob, a longtime friend of mine, began staying at home full time with his two preschool kids after his wife's promotion prompted them to relocate to a new city. Rob loved the amount of time he was able to spend with his two children, but this longtime "career guy" frequently struggled with his role and purpose. "Part of the struggle was my sense of worth," he reflected, "but I think most of it was simply not having a creative outlet at home."

Rob eventually decided to return to work, but his stay-at-home time convinced him that any job he would take would need to fit into his family priorities. As a result, instead of returning to an office environment all day, Rob had the luxury of waiting until he could find a position that allowed him to work from home much of the week. In the end, Rob was able to turn the catch–22 on its heels.

As Rob shows, a major factor in solving this problem

is the amount of flexibility a man has in his job. If he telecommutes or has flex time, he is ideally positioned to provide without sacrificing an involved role with his family. If a man's job is not flexible, he needs to consider prayerfully other alternatives to the all-or-nothing Provide versus Lead dilemma.

Finally, one of the biggest misconceptions of the Provider Dad mind-set is believing that the act of providing is a man's purpose in life. "Bringing home the bacon" is a man's responsibility, but it is not his calling. In fact, viewing the provider role as a calling can be downright dangerous. For when a man does so, he can justify the costs of a career (workaholic tendencies, constant business travel, little energy at home) in the name of Christian service. Instead, a man's leadership of his family is at the heart of his true calling and purpose.

But I am getting ahead of myself. I must first tell you about a place called Khumbu Icefall.

CHAPTER 6

TIGHTROPE DISCIPLESHIP

Jesus knows only one possibility:
simple surrender and obedience,
not interpreting it or applying it,
but doing and obeying it.
That is the only way to hear his word.
But again he does not mean that it is
to be discussed as an ideal,
he really means us to get on with it.
—Dietrich Bonhoeffer

Every Everest climber knows that he has a daredevil tightrope walk to survive before the real climb up the mountain even begins. Just out of Base Camp en route to Camp 1, Everesters have to pass through the Khumbu Icefall—a place that traditionally kills as many people each year as the highest regions of the mountain. The icefall is a huge ice formation, colorfully described by veteran guide Ben Marshall as "a 2,000-vertical-foot jungle gym on steroids."

In order to traverse the deep crevasses of the icefall, expeditionary teams lay a series of aluminum ladders and ropes that serve as makeshift bridges. Climbers are required to hold onto the ropes and then balance themselves as they cross over—all the while being loaded down with a heavy backpack and wearing awkward crampons* on their feet.

If that isn't challenging enough, the ice structures themselves are highly unstable and unpredictable. Climbers must feel as though they have stumbled onto an Indiana Jones film set as they face a series of deadly obstacles. Massive ice towers can collapse unexpectedly. Ice boulders frequently fall down from the glacier above. Hidden crevasses and weak ice bridges can cave in, hurling a climber down a hundred feet or more.

The desperate image of a lone climber struggling to make it across the Khumbu Icefall reminds me of what I felt like trying to live as a Balanced Man. My arms were full of commitments—a laptop on one side and a family photo album in the other. My Bible study teaching materials were tucked inside of my right underarm and a pair of running shoes were draped over my shoulders. With their own individual centers of gravity, each of these items would tug at my arms and shoulders and throw me off balance. The prospect of trying to successfully navigate an icefall bridge with this baggage covering me was not just daunting, but out of the question. I might make it a step or two, but I would inevitably lose control if I continued on. The only way I could avoid falling was to start tossing things left and right in a frantic effort to regain my balance.

There is an alternative, however. Suppose I step back from the ladder, set everything on the ground, and go fetch a knapsack to carry them all. I could then repack all my belongings inside the backpack, zip it up, and firmly secure its shoulder straps and waist belt to my body. Once

---

* A *crampon* is a frame of metal spikes that attach to a climber's boots for gripping on the ice.

I am back on the ladder, I would no longer find myself weighed down by various individual entanglements; I'd have a single center of gravity and free hands to hold onto the rope and steady myself as I cross. The icefall crossing would still be challenging, but fully doable.

As you can see from this illustration, one of the constant frustrations I always had as a father and husband was the difficulty in managing commitments. My family, work, and church ministries so often wanted to pull me in separate directions. I could respond effectively to one or two, but never to all of them. Something had to give. I became convinced that there were only two options. I could throw off most of these commitments in a willy-nilly effort to survive. Or I had to discover a unifying purpose that would bring them all together to form a single center of gravity, so to speak.

The Four Callings
of a Man

Call me cynical, but "be true to yourself" is one of those inspirational messages I often hear in the media that nearly triggers my gag reflex. I think of a scene in *The Sandlot* in which Babe Ruth gives advice to a young fan: "Follow your heart, kid, and you'll never go wrong." The underlying assumption to this throwaway line is that the boy's dreams and emotions are the best determinants for his life's decisions, that his ultimate commitment should be to nothing but his own feelings. I am pretty sure I have never seen "be true to yourself," "follow your heart," or even "live your dreams" anywhere in my Bible. The reason is, of course, obvious—*be true to myself* is just a veiled way of saying *be preoccupied with myself.* Jesus Christ instead tells a man to be true to something else—his calling (Eph. 4:1).

Inside and outside the church, a man's "calling" is almost always associated with his profession or vocation; they are treated as synonyms, used interchangeably. A doctor's calling is the medical field. A professor's calling is the classroom. A soldier's calling is protecting his country. But while God may have called each of these men to their particular line of work, a man's calling is not limited to what he does from nine to five. From a biblical standpoint, a calling is relevant to any part of a man's life (1 Cor. 7:17, 20).

A calling, as I see it, is a distinct identity that a man takes on when he responds to a call of Jesus Christ. It is not merely something he does, a role he plays, or a different hat he wears. It is also far more than a specific responsibility, duty, or chore. Think about the way in which a squire became a knight in medieval times. If he proved himself worthy and skillful in battle, a squire responded to an invitation by his lord—a calling, if you will—and went through a knighting ceremony. The whole identity of this young man forever changed when he heard the honored words, "I dub thee Sir Knight." No longer a squire, he now began serving his lord with a new identity. Seen in this light, a man's calling is not what he does so much as who he is.

As Christians, we usually speak of a person's calling in the singular rather than plural. There's one specific task a believer is called to do, one primary reason why spiritual gifts are given to a person. However, this belief is not consistent with the Bible. God calls every Christian man to be an obedient disciple and a man of godly adventure, no matter what he does for a living or the ministries he is involved in at his church. And if a man is married or if he has children living at home, Christ calls him to even more. Let me explain.

An Obedient Disciple

> Jesus said to his disciples, "Whoever wants to be my disciple must deny themselves and take up their cross and follow me. For whoever wants to save their life will lose it, but whoever loses their life for me will find it." (Matt. 16:24–25)

Regardless of his career or marital status, Jesus Christ calls a man first and foremost to a life of discipleship. "If anyone would come after me," says Christ in Matthew 16:24, "he must deny himself and take up his cross and follow me" (NIV). When a man accepts this calling and decides to live like a believer, Christ challenges him to hold nothing back and surrender everything to him. While the term *surrender* can so easily roll off the tongue on a Sunday morning, actually pulling it off is far more challenging. Yet, when a man makes the decision to live out his life in single-minded obedience to Christ, his life will never be the same. Dietrich Bonhoeffer puts it like this:

> The old life is left behind, and completely surrendered. The disciple is dragged out of his relative security into a life of absolute insecurity (that is, in truth, into the absolute security and safety of the fellowship of Jesus), from a life which is observable and calculable … into a life where everything is unobservable and fortuitous … out of the realm of finite … into the realm of infinite possibilities (which is the one liberating reality).

Answering the call to discipleship is the essential starting point to becoming an Expeditionary Man. Unless a man is willing to live like a disciple, he will never have the courage to fully hand over the reins of his career and financial security to Christ. He will never be able to cast aside the middle-class values that permeate our culture and suburban churches. He will never be able to redefine his ideas of adventure to complement, rather than compete with, his responsibilities at home.

If I took a word-association test and was given the term *disciple*, my instant reaction would probably be to mutter the names of two heroes of mine—George Müller and Hudson Taylor. In my mind, these two men show how Christ is able to use devotion, faith, and prayer to transform ordinary people into extraordinary disciples. Their stories are worth telling, for they have had a profound impact on me—both positive and negative—in the years to come.*

Business as usual. George Müller was a nineteenth-century English evangelist who, in 1836, felt called by God to respond to the desperate needs of orphans in his hometown of Bristol. So he founded an orphanage, initially taking in thirty children in his home. God blessed his ministry, and Müller soon felt led to expand his efforts to care for more and more and more orphans. Over the next quarter century, he worked to establish a series of orphanages across England that, by 1870, housed over two thousand children.

As amazing as these statistics are, what separates George Müller from many other philanthropists and mis-

---

* In the vignettes on George Müller and Hudson Taylor, I do take some artistic license by adding dialogue to the stories for dramatic effect. However, the essential facts of the stories are accurate.

sionaries is *how* he built his entire orphanage support system: he relied completely on faith and prayer. When he first got married, he and his wife read Psalm 81:10 ("Open thy mouth wide, and I will fill it," KJV) and believed they could take that passage at face value. So they became determined to rely on God alone to provide for their needs. Because of this conviction, Müller never once made pleas for financial help to churches or individual believers; he simply prayed that God would move others to provide for their material necessities. Time and time again, when the orphanages ran out of money for food, God stepped in at the last moment and provided for them. One story, in particular, captures the practical reality of the faith that powered this Christian disciple.

Müller awakened early one morning with the full realization that he did not have any food or milk to give to the orphans at breakfast. The cupboards were completely bare after the evening meal from the night before, and he had no money to buy food. Undeterred, Müller went about his normal morning activities, fully confident that God would provide in time. While Müller was in his study doing devotions, he heard a gentle knock on the door. Peeking in, his wife said, "The kids are waking. I need to get ready for breakfast. What do you want me to do?"

George replied with a relaxed half-smile, "Business as usual, my dear."

Winking at her husband, Mrs. Müller shut the study door to give him a few more minutes of solitude before the busy day began. She then went into the kitchen and set the plates, bowls, and cups on the table. Within a few moments, the children began filtering in and gathering around the tables. However, unlike most mornings, the milk pitchers and food trays were noticeably absent from the impeccably set tables.

The children stood waiting for breakfast to begin when George entered the room. "Children, you know we must be in time for school," he said. Everyone bowed their heads for prayer. Lifting his hand, George continued, "Dear Father, we thank Thee for what Thou art going to give us to eat."

No sooner had he uttered that short prayer when they heard a knock on the door. When George opened it, a baker greeted him and then said, "Mr. Müller, I couldn't sleep last night. Somehow I felt you didn't have bread for breakfast and the Lord wanted me to send you some. So I got up at 2 a.m. and baked some fresh bread, and have brought it."

George warmly thanked the man and invited him to come inside to give the bread to his wife. Moments later while they were still handing out the bread, George heard a second knock on the door. When he opened it, he was greeted by a milkman. The milkman went on to say that his milk cart had broken down right in front of the orphanage. He asked George if he could give the children his cans of fresh milk so he could empty his wagon and repair it.

It is often said that no child under Müller's care ever missed a meal. That truth serves as a testimony to Müller's steadfast faith and God's willingness to be involved in the daily details of the lives of his disciples.

In the nick of time. Hudson Taylor was born a generation after Müller in nineteenth-century England. Unlike Müller, however, he did not stick around and serve God in his home country. Instead, he left when he was in his twenties to become a missionary to China. During his half century of service, he is reported to have brought over 18,000 Chinese people to faith. Author Ruth Tucker sums up his overall influence: "No other missionary in the nineteen centuries since the Apostle Paul has had a wider vision and has carried out a more systematized plan of evangelizing a broad geographical area than Hudson Taylor." His evangelistic successes in China are perhaps unrivaled, but what enabled him to be so effective as a foreign missionary was the single-minded obedience to Christ that he began before he ever left the shores of his native England.

When Taylor was twenty years old, he had already felt the call to go to China as a missionary. However, convinced that he needed medical training before going overseas, he landed a job as a doctor's apprentice for a physician in London. Taylor was to get paid a salary and boarding allowance every four months, but he discovered early on that the doctor was forgetful. Taylor constantly had to remind the doctor that it was his payday. But as time went on, Taylor decided that he needed to trust God to do the prompting rather than himself. This situation was an ideal test, Taylor believed, to determine whether he really had the battle-tested faith of a disciple that he would need to survive in China.

The next payday came along, and the doctor forgot again. Taylor held firm to his decision and simply prayed about it over the next couple of weeks. But after three weeks without any resolution, Taylor was down to his last coin, which he ended up giving away to a family in need. This act of charity left him with no money for food and the rent due the following day.

When Taylor woke up the next morning, he knew he was going to have to tell his landlord he didn't have any money for her. However, just before doing so, the post-man delivered an unsigned letter containing a single pair of gloves and a sovereign coin, which was worth four times as much as the money he'd given away the day be-fore. Taylor was jubilant; this gift would keep him afloat for a while longer.

Fast forward to two weeks later. Taylor was working late with his boss at the office on a Saturday evening. By this time, he was once again back in the same finan-cial straits as he was before—flat broke, with no money for food and rent due the next day. As he was restocking medical supplies, Hudson began to pray that God would flash "Payday! Payday!" across the mind of the doctor.

The doctor was in his office, getting his coat on to leave for the night. An overdue notice on his desk got his attention, however. He came into the supply room and asked Hudson, "Didn't I pay the supplier this month? I got a notice stating that it had not yet been paid."

"No, I don't think you ever did," replied Hudson.

"Okay, I'll get that paid on Monday," said the doc. He turned to leave the room, but suddenly stopped in his tracks. After a brief pause, he rubbed his hand over his forehead, as if to massage his memory. "Say, I don't think I ever paid you this period either, did I?"

Did you really say what I think you said? Hudson almost replied in jubilation. Catching himself, Hudson tried to reply nonchalantly, but only half succeeded, saying "No, sir, I am afraid you did not."

"My bloody memory," the doc replied shaking his head in disgust. "Don't get old, Hudson. Don't get old." The doctor looked inside of his wallet for money to pay his as-sistant, but realized that he had no cash on him.

"Hudson, I need to beg your indulgence for another

two days. I have to wait until the bank opens on Monday morning before I can pay you." With that, the doctor shut the door and left for the night, leaving Taylor to close up the office.

Taylor stood by himself in the empty office, bewildered, not exactly sure what to think. On the one hand, he was overjoyed that the long wait was over. On the other hand, news of the thirty-six-hour delay until he could receive the money really stung. Unless a miracle occurred, he knew he would go hungry tomorrow and be late on his rent. So he prayed again.

At 10:00 p.m., Taylor was getting ready to leave the office for the night when he heard the door abruptly open. He was a bit taken aback for a moment until he saw the familiar profile of the doctor hurriedly coming into the room.

"Is everything okay?" Taylor quickly asked, thinking that there must be some emergency. "Can I get your exam room . . . ," Hudson started to say, but his voice trailed off when he saw the doctor smiling and laughing.

"Sit down, sit down, Hudson," said the doctor chuckling. "You have got to hear the story of what just happened to me."

After Hudson found a chair, the doctor continued, "I was getting ready for bed right about nine o'clock, when I suddenly heard a knock at the door. I opened it, wondering who it could possibly be at that late hour on a Saturday night. Lo and behold, it was one of my long-time patients, Roger Thomas. For some unknown reason, he insisted on paying his bill tonight. Roger always settles his account by cheque, but he wanted to pay in cash this time."

After chuckling some more about the absurdity of it all, the doctor took the money out from his pocket and gave it to Taylor as his paycheck. "We're all settled now," the doctor said.

"All settled," Hudson said, breathing a huge sigh of relief.

The two locked the office door and headed off into the night in separate directions. All the way home, Taylor smiled as he thanked God for coming through for him, once again providing everything he needed in just the nick of time.

Not everyone is called to run a series of orphanages or to travel to China as a missionary. But a man is called to live his life with the same rock-solid faith as Müller and Taylor regardless of whether or not God provides for him in the same way that he did to those two men. Both were able to lay everything on the line for Christ because they trusted fully in him.

The term *disciple* is used so loosely today that we tend to use it to refer to anyone who comes to church on a Sunday morning. But, as Müller and Taylor show, the decision to live a life of discipleship is every bit as significant as a squire's transformation into a knight. It's a different life. Listen to Bonhoeffer explain the impact that Christ's call to discipleship had on Matthew and Peter:

> So long as Levi sits at the receipt of custom, and Peter at his nets, they could both pursue their trade honestly and dutifully, and they might both enjoy religious experiences, old and new. But if they want to believe in God, the only way is to follow his incarnate Son.
>
> Until that day, everything had been different. They could remain in obscurity, pursuing their work as the quiet in the land, observing the law and waiting for the coming of the Messiah. But now he has come, and

his call goes forth. Faith can no longer mean sitting still and waiting—they must rise and follow him ... They must burn their boats and plunge into absolute insecurity in order to learn the demand and the gift of Christ. Had Levi stayed at his post, Jesus might have been his present help in trouble, but not the Lord of his whole life.

A Man of Godly Adventure

> I urge you to live a life worthy of the calling you have received. (Eph. 4:1)

No matter a man's profession or situation in life, God calls every Christian man to live a life of godly adventure. A man instinctively knows this. To borrow a line from C. S. Lewis, "We do not merely observe men, we *are* men. In this case we have, so to speak, inside information; we are in the know." Every man, therefore, has "inside information" that helps him sense that he is called to some sort of adventure, even if he is unsure what it might be.

Since the Bible never talks about "adventure" by name, some may be tempted to dismiss this calling as a postmodern redux. I disagree. Look closely at Ephesians 4:1: "Therefore I, the prisoner of the Lord, implore you to walk in a manner worthy of the calling with which you have been called" (NASB). Notice the "therefore" in this verse, connecting chapter 4 to the first three chapters of Ephesians. Read in the context of the entire letter, Paul is telling us to take stock of all the spiritual blessings we have received—the free gift of grace, the unity of believers, and the Holy Spirit at work within us—and then live up to these gifts. The faith we display on the outside, says Paul, should be consistent with everything we can claim as true in our hearts and minds.

With that backdrop, the term "godly adventure" starts to make much more sense. "Adventure" is, after all, defined by *American Heritage Dictionary* as "an undertaking of a hazardous nature" and by WordNet as a "wild and exciting undertaking." These definitions seem to describe perfectly what a man's life will be like if he faithfully lives out Ephesians 4:1 — living by uncompromising principle and unbridled passion doing whatever God calls him to.

Over two thousand years of church history speak to the reality of godly adventurers, including martyrs, defenders of orthodoxy, church protesters, Bible smugglers, missionaries, Christian explorers, and civil rights leaders, only to name a few. In fact, consider the words that Christ spoke to his disciples just before his ascension into heaven: "Therefore go and make disciples of all nations, baptizing them in the name of the Father and of the Son and of the Holy Spirit, and teaching them to obey everything I have commanded you" (Matt. 28:19–20). When you consider the practical considerations of living out that verse, the Great Commission suddenly becomes a Great Christian Adventure.

A Serving Husband

Husbands, love your wives, just as Christ loved the church and gave himself up for her to make her holy, cleansing her by the washing with water through the word, and to present her to himself as a radiant church, without stain or wrinkle or any other blemish, but holy and blameless. In this same way, husbands ought to love their wives as their own bodies. He who loves his wife loves himself. (Eph. 5:25–28)

If a man is married, he is called to love his wife in the same manner in which Christ loved the church (Eph. 5:25).

The metaphor Paul uses can hardly be more potent. Christ's love is demonstrated through his total and complete sacrifice to the church, giving himself up and laying down his life for her (John 15:13). In the same way, a man is called to sacrifice his own life for his wife. Sometimes that means giving up a career opportunity or a recreational activity that consumes too much of his time and attention. Most of the time, however, a man's sacrificial agape love is expressed by serving, encouraging, honoring, and supporting his wife on a day-in, day-out basis.

When a man and his wife have a healthy, growing marriage, the relationship inevitably impacts the spiritual and emotional development of their children. "The most important thing a father can do for his children is to love their mother," Theodore Hesburgh once said. I am not sure if that is necessarily scriptural, but it is probably pretty close.

For married men, the life of an Expeditionary Man is built on the marital unity and intimacy of a man and his wife. Together, they need to be the reliable core of the team that is ready to ascend the mountain.

Sometimes the best illustrations come from the most unlikely of places. Judging by its title, Adam Sandler's film *Fifty First Dates* sounds like the last place you would look for profound meaning on relationships. And yet, more than perhaps any film I've seen in years, *Fifty First Dates* offers an amazing portrayal of what agape love really is.

Adam Sandler plays Henry Roth, a man who is completely self-absorbed. Living on Maui, Henry has a fondness for dating tourists, because he knows he will never have to deal with long-term commitments. However, one morning when he is taking out his boat for a sail, a mechanical problem strands him at a cafe. During break-fast, Henry ends up sitting and eating with a woman named Lucy, whom he immediately develops a crush on. The two of them hit it off well, so Henry decides to return to the cafe the next morning to see her again and ask her out.

However, when he comes to the table to flirt with her, she does not recognize him and, in fact, becomes upset at Henry's forwardness. Henry is speechless and cannot understand what is going on—that is, until the restaurant owner grabs him and pulls him outside to explain the story. Lucy, he discovers, was in a severe auto accident on her father's birthday last year and now suffers from a permanent neurological condition known as Goldfield Syndrome. While her long-term memory is normal, she is unable to retain short-term memory beyond a day. As a result, every time she wakes up in the morning, Lucy believes she is waking up on her father's birthday, the day of the accident. Her slate is wiped clean, so to speak.

When Henry talks with his best friend about it, he encourages Henry to date Lucy. She'd be the perfect woman for Henry, his friend reasons, because he would never have to worry about a long-term commitment. Henry is beginning to fall in love with Lucy and doesn't even think about taking advantage of her like that. Yet, in spite of the hopelessness of the situation, Henry just cannot stay away.

And so, day after day, Henry goes to be with Lucy, care for her, and win her love over and over and over again. Throughout the process, you begin to see a deep change taking place inside him. He is slowly being transformed from a completely reprehensible, selfish man into a self-less, loving servant. Lucy's father and brother are content to try and artificially remake the day of the crash, so she doesn't have to deal with the trauma of her condition. However, Henry is the one who realizes that this deception hurts more than it helps, and so he comes up with the idea of using a video tape and diary to help Lucy deal each new day with the fallout of the accident. As Henry begins to work with her father and brother to care for her, his life starts to completely revolve around her.

Fast forward to the end of the film, and Henry, after much drama, ends up marrying Lucy. Regardless, every morning, she continues to wake up to the memory of her father's birthday so many years before. Henry is once asked by a friend, "So every day you help her realize what happened and you wait patiently for her to be okay with it. And then you get her to fall in love with you again?" One can imagine the ongoing sacrifice required to do that each and every day. His needs are always going to be in second place. He must spend his energy on her doing the same things over and over again with no chance of long-term improvement.

The book of Lamentations (3:22–23) tells us that God's mercies are new every morning. In the same way, as Henry Roth shows us, a man's love for his wife should be renewed every morning as he devotes himself to her with such dedication that she cannot help but fall in love once again. That's the calling of a serving husband.

A Hands-On Father

> Start children off on the way they should go, and even when they are old they will not turn from it. (Prov. 22:6)

When the Bible speaks of fatherhood, there is an underlying assumption of a father being personally involved

in the training and discipling of his children. I have already pointed to several scriptural teachings, but there
are even more to discuss. In Deuteronomy 6:5–7, Moses
ties together a man's love for God with his responsibility
to instill that same love in his children:

> Love the LORD your God with all your heart and
> with all your soul and with all your strength. These
> commandments that I give you today are to be on your
> hearts. Impress them on your children. Talk about
> them when you sit at home and when you walk along
> the road, when you lie down and when you get up.

Moses doesn't mince words in this passage. You *must*
teach them. You *must* speak of them—not just on Sunday mornings, but on a constant, ongoing basis around the
home. A few chapters later in Deuteronomy 11:18–21,
Moses reiterates the need for fathers to constantly disciple
their children:

> Fix these words of mine in your hearts and minds;
> tie them as symbols on your hands and bind them on
> your foreheads. Teach them to your children, talking
> about them when you sit at home and when you walk
> along the road, when you lie down and when you get
> up. Write them on the doorframes of your houses
> and on your gates, so that your days and the days of
> your children may be many in the land that the LORD
> swore to give your ancestors, as many as the days that
> the heavens are above the earth.

This biblical message to fathers is not just an Old Testament teaching either. In his letter to the Ephesians, Paul
affirms the teaching of Deuteronomy by instructing the
men of Ephesus to raise their children in the "training and
instruction of the Lord" (Eph. 6:4). One cannot escape

the hands-on nature of biblical fatherhood in the Scriptures, the calling of a man to be personally involved in all phases of his children's spiritual development.

One Unified Purpose

I have a single-focused personality. When I have several projects on my plate, my natural response is to focus all of my attention on one of them, work on it until the job is done right, and then move on to the next. Obviously, in the real world, I am rarely able to do that, so I usually have a constant competition running through my mind over which one gets my attention at a given point in time.

I think back to when I was leading an engineering division at an Internet software company. In this role, I wore several hats—the engineering guru to the marketing director, the budget and schedule manager to my boss, the employee manager to my staff, and final decision maker and arbiter on the engineering team. The challenge I had was providing sufficient attention to each of these roles so that I could match the need and expectations of others involved. Given the hectic environment of the company, I could easily fall into reactive mode, playing fireman to the inevitable fires that arose in one of these areas rather than carefully prioritizing and managing the responsibilities across all the parts of the division.

It's not surprising, then, that when I look at the callings to be a disciple, adventurous man, husband, and father, I see competition written all over the place. A disciple is out there evangelizing the masses. A man of godly adventure is working his tail off serving God by doing what he loves. A servant-like husband is sacrificing himself to ensure his wife's needs are met. A hands-on father is spending quality time with his children. If I am really going to live out each of these callings to the fullest, won't each demand all of my time, energy, and focus? Won't their purposes and agendas constantly compete?

From a human standpoint, these commitments certainly appear destined to step all over each other. But when I consider these questions in light of Scripture, I am convinced of the exact opposite—that they are designed by God to complement, not compete against, each other. My conviction is based on one underlying factor: they all originate from a common source, Jesus Christ. If Jesus Christ is giving a man four different callings, they must fit together toward a unified purpose. If not, Christ would be setting a man up for failure—handing out too much to do without giving him enough resources to pull it off. He would be much like an out-of-touch boss who gives his secretary a handful of disparate, time-consuming tasks to do just before the start of an important board meeting.

A man is called to disciple others, serve his wife, train his children, and live an adventuresome purpose. But only when he is fully focused on his family is he free to live out each of these callings without constant competition. Seen in this light, a man's principal purpose, while his children are inside his home, becomes obvious—to make his family his primary mission field.

The Puritans understood long ago how these four callings worked together for a man. When we talk of the Puritans today, we usually focus most of our attention on their social and political attitudes. But looming over these issues in the Puritan worldview was always the centrality of the family. "If the family failed to teach its members properly," says historian Edmund Morgan, "neither the state nor the church could be expected to accomplish much." As a result, a Puritan man's foremost calling was to his family.

The Puritans even referred to the family as a "little church." Or, as Puritan pastor Lewis Bayly put it, "what the preacher is in the pulpit, the same the Christian householder is in his house." Along that same line, John Cotton wrote *The Way of Life* (1641), in which he talked about how a man's covenant relationship with God was tied to the spiritual life of his family. He said, "If God made a Covenant, to be a God to thee and thine, then it is thy part to see it, that thy children and servants be God's people."

Contrast that attitude with today's world. When a man today thinks of his "little church," he is probably not thinking of his family. So too, when a man considers his mission field, his kids are not usually at the top of the list. Instead, his natural response is to think about people he can impact in the world outside of his home—his neighbors, coworkers, homeless at the soup kitchen, or people in Africa or elsewhere in the world. He usually takes it for granted that the faith of his children is something he can count on.

A quick peek at world history, however, will tell us how shortsighted this line of thinking can be. Think about the many failed empires from yesteryear. One of their tendencies was an insatiable hunger to expand an empire's borders in a quest for more and more territory. But the rulers fell into the inevitable trap of spreading themselves too fast and too thin and, in so doing, neglecting the needs of their citizens. Consequently, the downfall of these kingdoms came, not from invading enemies from afar, but from revolts within. The lesson learned is simple: *secure your homeland, and then and only then, expand your territory.*

Noah and Eli are two men from the Old Testament whose lives poignantly demonstrate this principle. Their lasting legacy on the world is directly proportional to their focus on home. One man made his family his primary mission field and the other did not.

Scripture does not tell us much about the life of Noah before the flood, only that he was a righteous man called by God to build an ark. But looking at the faith of his three boys named Shem, Ham, and Japheth, we do know that he trained and instructed them in the knowledge of God and his ways. I can envision Noah working alongside them for years as they built the ark together. While he did so, he probably used the time as an opportunity to talk about his faith and the coming judgment. Given the rampant sin in the world at the time, I am sure that the peer pressure on Shem, Ham, and Japheth growing up was considerable as others mocked their father's building project. But, like their father, they remained faithful and God delivered them.

What's more, consider how God used Noah's three sons in his earthly plan — they were the exclusive link between the pre- and post-flood worlds to populate the earth. I shudder to think of what would have happened if Noah had neglected his family and not discipled his boys; only God knows what would have happened to planet Earth.

Living over a millennium after Noah, Eli was an Israelite priest and judge who served ancient Israel for forty years. He was evidently a well-meaning guy in his role as priest at Shiloh. But he never took his calling as a father seriously enough to pass his faith onto his two boys, Hophni and Phinehas. Perhaps he believed that his position in the tabernacle ensured that they would follow suit.

But Eli's sons had no interest in sincere faith. Put to work by their father at the tabernacle, they got involved in a lot of nasty business, even going so far as to take meat that was intended as sacrificial offerings and to eat it themselves. Eli either looked the other way for many years or was so preoccupied with his job that he did not even notice what was going on around him. It was not until others came to him complaining about his sons' actions that he rebuked Hophni and Phinehas. But it was too little, too late. God soon struck down Eli's sons in battle and Eli died shortly thereafter. Samuel, who was living with Eli at the time, emerged as a prophet/priest, while Eli's family vanished into obscurity.

In the end, Noah left a lasting legacy that changed the world. Eli, on the other hand, left no legacy at all. Looking back, the key difference between these two men of God was related to their dedication and focus at home.

MYTH OF OTHER DAYS

None of the four callings of a man have expiration dates associated with them. A man will always be called to be a disciple and a man of godly adventure no matter his age or walk in life. So long as his wife is living, a man is called to continue as a serving, sacrificing husband. And even when a man's children are fully grown, he is still called to teach and train them (and his grandchildren), even if he only sees them occasionally.

However, there is one aspect of fatherhood that differentiates it from the other three—its dependence on time. It peaks and then subsides. Fatherhood floods into a man's life when his first child is born and takes it over, dropping off only when his last kid leaves home as an adult.

For the majority of men, this peaking of activity is just a small portion of their adult lives. But when a man is in the midst of it, he does not often think that way. Instead, he starts believing in the Myth of Other Days, thinking that this season of life will last forever. Charles Francis Adams was one such man.

CHAPTER 7

WINDOWS OF OPPORTUNITY

An adventure is, by its nature,
a thing that comes to us.
It is a thing that chooses us,
not a thing we choose.
—G. K. Chesterton

It was the best of times; it was the worst of times. It just depended on whom you were talking to. Charles Francis Adams was a prominent political figure during the mid-nineteenth century. Politics was in his bloodline—he was, after all, the grandson of President John Adams. But it was also his passion. Armed with a Puritan's work ethic and sense of duty, Charles believed his time and energy should be devoted to public service and government. His résumé speaks to his devotion—Massachusetts state representative, state senator, vice presidential nominee, congressman, and U.S. ambassador to Britain during the Lincoln administration. Charles was the father of four sons, but given his preoccupation with work, he was not around his family that much.

Because the members of the Adams family were regular journalers, we know that on at least one occasion he managed to take his eight-year-old son Brook fishing. Brook was deeply affected by the experience and wrote in his diary about this father-son outing when he returned home that evening: "Went fishing with my father—the most wonderful day of my life!"

When I first read Brook's account, I thought that Charles, as busy as he was, was able to relax and enjoy the brief time away with his son and give him his full attention. Perhaps Charles even got a bit misty-eyed thinking about how quickly Brook was growing up. But when I dove further into the story, I discovered I was wrong. Charles may have been pleasant enough with his son, but his mind was somewhere else. He logged this entry into his diary for that day: "Went fishing with my son today—a day wasted." Clearly, Charles would have rather been at the office getting work done than fishing with his son.

As the story of Charles Francis Adams shows, the years of fatherhood come at the most inconvenient time for a man. He begins to grow his family at around the same age in which he builds his career. It is not long before the boundary lines are set for the battle over his heart. A playpen or a promotion. Diapers or dollars. Noogies or networking. Happy Meals or hobnobbing.

For many men, the deck is stacked against the family at this stage of their lives. The potential of a man's career is too seductive to resist. He is beyond the entry level jobs of his mid-twenties, through with postgraduate programs, and on the verge of peaking professionally. He retains a youthful bravado and energy, but now has experience to back it up. In the back of his mind, he senses he is approaching the "make-it-or-break-it" point in his career. Based on his performance over the next few years, he will continue to rise in his profession and gain prominence or end up plateauing into a midlevel existence. With this pressure and purpose, few men are prone to be reflective or contemplative about their family at this stage of their lives. The kids, after all, are still in diapers or just entering school. *I'll have plenty of time for them once I am established*, he reasons.

Remember the scene in *Field of Dreams* in which Ray Kinsella asks Doc "Moonlight" Graham about his one shining moment in major league baseball—playing in one inning of one game. Graham was sent up from the minor leagues to the New York Giants three weeks before the end of the season. In spite of his initial excitement over the chance to prove himself, he rode the bench the entire time—that is, until the final inning of the final game. "Graham," shouts the manager. "Right field." Graham eagerly dashes out to his position hoping at last to make a play. But three quick outs later, the ball never even makes it out of the infield, bringing an end to the season and his best shot at the majors.

Unable to bear the thought of being sent back down to the minors the next season, Graham decided to retire and become a doctor. As Graham shares with Ray his memories, he looks back at his life and says, "You know, we just don't recognize the most significant moments of our lives while they're happening. Back then I thought, well, there'll be other days. I didn't realize that that was the only day."

In this scene, I love the way Moonlight Graham nails it—he perfectly captures something I call the Myth of Other Days that dogs so many men. When a man has kids growing up in his home, time goes by quickly—but not that quickly. When the kids are young, the moments really do seem like they will last forever. He can easily lull himself into believing that "there'll be other days," once he takes care of business.

Maybe it is the life-or-death reality of the setting, but Everest climbers do not fall victim to these kinds of myths and procrastinations. They know that the secret of conquering Everest is timing. It matters little when the climbing team would like to go or what is most convenient for their schedule. Instead, it's the weather that dictates the summit attempt.

For over 250 days a year, Everest is held hostage by violent, hurricane-force winds from the jet stream that savage the peak with bursts up to two hundred miles per hour. Not to be outdone, storm clouds rise from the surrounding valleys to barrage the mountain with snow. No climber would ever try for the summit in this weather or he would literally be blown off the mountain. However, twice a year, during the months of May and September, Everest is granted a reprieve. Warm monsoon air comes from the south to push the jet stream high over the summit, creating a short, calm window of ideal climbing weather. These weather windows last only a handful of days, but they produce clear skies and winds as little as five miles per hour.

As an expedition team acclimatizes for several weeks, its leader uses satellite and Internet technology to continuously monitor meteorological reports. His job is to locate a five-day window of stable weather and then correctly position his team on the mountain to be able to make a summit attempt once an exact date and time is set. An experienced leader keeps an eye on the meteorological forecasts but knows there are local weather systems on the mountains that the reports cannot predict. In the end, the leader has to develop a natural instinct for when to go and when to stay. He risks the lives of every member of the team if he is gung-ho and cavalier. At the same time, he cannot afford to wait until the "perfect" conditions come along either. Since his team is waiting at extreme altitude, they grow physically weaker as time goes on. If the leader holds out too long, the team will lose any opportunity to go for the summit.

The weather window on Everest parallels the short season of life that a man has to spend time with and influence his children. Like an Everest climber, he is not free to decide when it is most convenient to play dad. His children do. If he waits too long, he will miss his chance; his window of opportunity will close forever. This is normally a private issue between a man and his family. But if you happened to see PBS's 2002 miniseries *Frontier House*, you had a chance to witness a man's window of opportunity open and close before your eyes—right on national television.

BACK TO THE FUTURE

Gordon Clune is the successful president of a multimillion-dollar manufacturing business in Hollywood, California. His family of five, along with his niece, was one of three families selected for a PBS reality television series that explored whether or not a family from the twenty-first century could make it on the American West frontier in the year 1883. Each of the homesteading families agreed to live without modern conveniences and technologies as they battled heat, blizzards, hunger, and themselves in order to survive.

Gordon was particularly excited for the five-month-long adventure as a way to bring his family together. "I guess I've been a little bit of a workaholic," confessed

Gordon before they left for Montana. "And I've been traveling. And I spend a lot of time taking care of business. And I'm not spending as much time sometimes with my family. And they're at that critical age where if I blink it's too late. They're gonna be gone."

When they first arrived on the frontier, the Clunes had a difficult time adjusting to an 1883 lifestyle. In fact, when watching them, I had a flashback to the kids in the film *Willy Wonka and the Chocolate Factory*, who whined and complained during the Wonka tour. Everyone in the Clune family was preoccupied with food and had difficulty rationing out their supplies. Gordon was frustrated carrying water 150 feet to the cabin, despite the fact that this distance was typical for homesteaders. Gordon's wife, Adrienne, and the girls complained about not being able to wear makeup. "Pure Hollywood" was the initial reaction of the other homesteaders to the Clunes.

Yet, as the weeks passed by, I began to notice a change gradually sweeping through the family. As times got tougher, the Clunes were pulling together. They worked as a family to grow food crops and raise livestock. They scrambled as a team to quickly build a fence to keep grazing cattle from destroying their crops. "Sometimes the wolf at the door is a good thing to make you all band together," Gordon said. Oh, they still often portrayed a spoiled attitude, had occasional rifts with the other homesteaders, and even got caught breaking the show rules on two occasions. But, in spite of these issues, each of the Clunes was thinking about himself or herself less and less and doing more and more tasks selflessly for the family. Rudy Brooks, one of the other homesteaders, noticed something going on too. In one of the "talking head" interviews, Rudy observed that the Clunes were the family who were changing the most through the experience. "They are a family growing closer," he said.

As I watched the series, I was particularly struck by a scene that seemed to capture the heart of the New and Improved Clunes: an afternoon picnic together. On a warm sunny day, the camera showed a family in an open meadow having a great time relaxing, laughing, and talking together. *They never would have done that back in Hollywood*, I thought to myself.

In a talking head interview, Gordon expressed his excitement about the changes taking place: "I've completely connected with them. And they appreciate me more and I appreciate them more. And I just love them tremendously. A lot more than I probably ever could have, because of the experiences that we've grown together, and doing together here."

On the final morning of the *Frontier House* experience, the cameras tracked the Clunes as they closed the door on their cabin and began walking away together toward modern civilization. Their days on the frontier were history, but there was so much promise of permanent change in all that had transpired. *Wait! What happens next when they go home?* I begged the television for answers.

The closing moments of the *Frontier House* series gave me the answers I was looking for. The show caught up with each of the homesteading families two months after the experience was over. As I waited for the segment showing the Clunes, I was nervous. Did Gordon alter his work habits so he could be more involved at home? Did the family make major lifestyle changes as a result of what they went through?

When the Clune segment began, my hopeful excitement turned into a sick feeling in my stomach. The camera showed a multimillion-dollar, seaside mansion in Malibu that was built for the Clunes while they were away in Montana. The camera then panned over to Gordon, all decked out in an Armani-like suit, walking out a set of massive, fifteen-foot-high mahogany wood front doors. Was I watching *Frontier House* or *The Lifestyles of the Rich and Famous*? The Clune mansion was spectacular, but it had an eerie, soulless quality to it.

Of all the Clunes, Adrienne was the person most eager to leave 1883 behind and return to modern America. However, during the interview, she was visibly uncomfortable in their new home. She seemed to long for the intimacy and coziness of the cabin. As she continued, her eyes revealed a deep loneliness, missing her traveling husband and feeling alienated from her kids spread out through the house.

Even Gordon did not seem to be enjoying his new house that much. His workload and travel demands were greater than ever, so he was never home. He lamented the fact that, unlike his time on the frontier, he was working hard in a world that his kids had no clue about. "It's seamless, they're isolated from it," said Gordon. "And I realize that more so than ever since I've been back."

As the credits began to roll on the series, I felt like I had just watched a Greek tragedy played out before my eyes. Some men fail to recognize the ticking clock until it is too late. However, Gordon was different. Before the *Frontier House* experience, he understood that his workaholic tendencies were taking him away from his family and he hoped that the frontier would bring them together. He got his wish. "For five months back in 1883, I got more satisfaction, more accomplishment, more appreciation than I did in my entire career beforehand." But in the end, it didn't matter. Gordon blinked, and he went back to business as usual.

I turned off the television and began wondering what Gordon would think about his decision twenty years from now. As I did so, a chilling line from C. S. Lewis's *The Screwtape Letters* kept echoing through my head: "I now see that I spent most of my life in doing neither what I ought nor what I liked."

MOIST CLAY

It does not have to be this way for a man. For a time, God gives a man a window of opportunity to enjoy his children and train them. But it is only a brief window. J. C. Ryle, a nineteenth-century Anglican bishop, understood this well:

> He gives your children a mind that will receive impressions like moist clay. He gives them a disposition at the starting-point of life to believe what you tell them, and to take for granted what you advise them, and to trust your word rather than a stranger's. He gives you, in short, a golden opportunity of doing them good. See that the opportunity be not neglected, and thrown away. Once let slip, it is gone for ever.

As Ryle suggests, God grants a man several years to mold and shape the hearts and minds of his children. During this stage, they instinctively trust their father and believe what he tells them. Then, as they grow older and become more independent, he has a final opportunity to influence them.

In the *Frontier House* miniseries, a talking head interview with Conner Clune, the youngest son of Gordon, shows the "moist clay" that lies in the heart of every child. In the segment, Conner is beaming as he talks about how much he loves the time that he is able to spend with his dad on the frontier. Back in California, Conner rarely saw his dad more than once or twice a week. In fact, by the time Gordon normally arrived home from work, Conner was already in bed. "He's always doing his business things," said Conner. As the nine-year-old Conner talked into the camera about how much he loved learning from his father, I could see a boy who just wanted to be molded by his dad:

> I learn better with my dad ... now he teaches me a whole bunch of more things like how to fish better, how to cast, tie my own hooks and things like that. And I just think it's better for that to happen, because I don't get a chance for him to teach me things back at home. I just want him to like teach me more things. And I want to be just like him when I grow up.

This influence of a father can be clearly seen in matters of faith as he shapes and molds his kids from infancy to adulthood. In his book *Soul Searching: The Religious and Spiritual Lives of American Teenagers*, author Christian Smith reveals that parents are the most significant factor influencing the spiritual lives of adolescents, even though the parents may not realize it. According to his research, the value that a parent places on faith roughly corresponds to the value that the child also places on faith. When faith is "extremely important" to the parents, 67 percent of adolescents said that faith is extremely or very important to them as well. "We get what we are," concludes Smith.

These statistics sound encouraging, but they have to be

juxtaposed against the Barna Research study I mentioned in chapter 3 — the one that discovered that 60 percent of kids who grow up in Christian homes end up leaving their faith by the time they are in their twenties. I am struck by the seeming inconsistency in research. How can parental influence be so profound for adolescents and yet be forgotten when the same kids grow into adults? The only explanation is that the influence of the majority of Christian parents is paper-thin, producing only temporary, not long-term decisions. In order to have a lasting influence, a man needs to do more than profess his faith in his home and train them from afar. A man needs "street cred" with his children.

STREET CRED

When kids are young, they usually give a free pass to their dads. Despite the workaholic tendencies of their fathers, Conner Clune and Brook Adams both gave their fathers the benefit of the doubt and made the best of it. They could deal with their dad's work without resentment and still be open to him. But when these young kids grow older and enter their teen years, these fathers will begin to lose all their credibility. The halo effect will leave the father, and they will start to write him off. To prevent this from happening, a man needs to play an increasingly hands-on leadership role the older his children get to remain a steady, lasting influence on their lives. Kids need to see a genuine commitment from their father, or they will dismiss him.

In the corporate world, I've been in work environments in which an out-of-touch executive does a periodic sweep through the office, getting all chummy with employees, and trying to get their buy-in on a new venture. It never works. The worker bees roll their eyes and wait patiently for the executive to go back into the cave from which he came. However, contrast those lame attempts with the strategy of my former CEO, Sam. Sam had a brilliant way of keeping in tune with all parts of the company. He would regularly join in with the QA folks beta-testing the software when a key deadline approached, sit in with engineering on planning sessions, play Ping Pong with others at lunch time — that sort of thing. Later, when Sam needed the company employees to get behind a new direction or ensure that a key shipping date was met, he had the "street cred" needed to pull it off. The employees knew they had a leader who understood them and, in turn, the kind of leader they could relate to and wanted to follow.

U.S. General George Patton, made famous as a field general during World War II, understood this principle of leadership perfectly. He was a master at leading, influencing, and motivating his troops. Rather than hanging out with the crusty old generals, he was often found at the front, swapping stories with commonplace GIs. Throughout World War II, he demonstrated the role of servant leader. Soldiers tell of a time when he was riding in a jeep and came across a sentry's vehicle stuck in the snow. Patton yelled at the sentries to get out and push, and before they knew it, they found Patton pushing and getting covered with snow alongside them. "A soldier's leader" is the affectionate phrase that one private used to describe him.

To Patton, street cred was more than just a leadership technique. He genuinely liked investing in the lives of those he led. In the same way, as a man invests more and more time with his children, he'll increasingly love what he does. "A day wasted," as Charles Adams put it, will be transformed into "a day blessed."

Patton was highly influenced by Civil War general William Tecumseh Sherman, who followed many of these same practices when he led his troops. Sherman wrote in his memoirs about the importance of hands-on leadership:

> Some men think that modern armies may be so regulated that a general can sit in an office and play on his several columns as on the keys of a piano; this is a fearful mistake. The directing mind must be at the very head of the army—must be seen there, and the effect of his mind and personal energy must be felt by every office and man present with it, to secure best results.

If I wordsmith this quote to make it more applicable to fathers, it would go something like this: *Some men think that the responsibility of Proverbs 22:6 can be accomplished by sitting in their offices, serving on church committees, and fathering in their spare time; this is a fatal mistake. As a servant leader, the man must be at the very head of the family—must be seen there, and the effect of his mind and personal energy must be felt by his children and wife, to make a lasting difference.*

Andy Reese may have never read Sherman's book, but he is one man who is following Sherman's advice with his teenage children. He has street cred; his kids actually care about what he thinks. *Does he like their favorite video game? Does he like the film they just watched? How many iTunes stars would Andy rate the song they played him?*

Andy's children do things with their friends, of course, but they genuinely like to hang out together as a family, whether it is a movie night at home or a trip to the mall. When, for example, he had to chauffeur his kids to a bowling outing and later a movie, they asked Andy to join with them. At age 15, I certainly never thought of doing that with my father when I was going out with my friends.

Having an open relationship with their father, Andy's children respond to him as well. They actually take an interest in his job. "What's your next project, Dad?" They rally to support him during crunch time. "Did you make your deadline?" they ask.

Because of the street cred Andy has established in their lives, they respond to him rather than resent him or rebel against him when he challenges them, whether in school, chores, or their relationship with Christ.

Many parents scoff that these sorts of responses are impossible for a "normal teen." *Andy's children are either weird or truly special*, they dismiss. But if you say that to Andy, he would shake his head with a gentle smile: "They may be wonderful kids, but they are as imperfect and sin-natured as any other average teen. We still struggle with each of them at times. But as we work through these battles together, they remain open and have never shut us out."

THE JARRING REMINDER

It was 3:20 a.m. Kim was working the night shift in the neonatal ICU down in Worcester, so I was using the open night as a productive late-writing session. However, by this point I was getting sleepy, so I took a two-minute break to wake up. I walked upstairs to check to see if the boys left the bathroom light on, and then peeked in on them as they were sound asleep in their beds. Each of them looked so big. I found myself performing a sort of ritual—I breathed in as deep a breath as I could manage, held it in my lungs for a second or two, and then slowly exhaled until the air completely left my lungs. *Suck it in, Rich*, I told myself. *Enjoy this moment for as long as you can.* This exercise was a reminder to be grateful for right now—that my boys are still living in my home, that I still get to enjoy them, and that I still have an opportunity to have an impact on them before they leave home for college and career.

After savoring that moment, I closed the bedroom doors and returned downstairs to my office to continue working on my manuscript. But as I looked at my monitor, I could not help but glance over to the stack of bills piled high on the corner of my desk. It was a jarring reminder that the hands-on role I am currently playing with my boys comes at a cost to my career and ability to provide.

It's easy to talk about all of this Expeditionary Man stuff in a vacuum, without any risk in the real world. Yet, as I found, when a man actually takes these steps, he is certain to enter the "Death Zone."

CHAPTER 8

THRIVING IN THE DEATH ZONE

*It's a living hell. The only way to describe it is
an utter exhaustion. You really don't care if you die
or if you just sit down and don't go any further.*
— Everest climber Dave Carter

"How long to sing this song?" Bono sang out from my
iPod. I was jogging down Highway 62 about a mile from
my house, half listening to music, half crying out to God
about our frustrating situation. When anxiety comes,
people do a lot different things to cope—drink, sleep,
or shop, to name a few. I pray about it, of course, but I
also work out. Perhaps the physical exercise helps me deal
with the discouragement and frustration. Or maybe I am
just subconsciously trying to outrun the problems that
loom over me.

The third-year anniversary of my move into full-time
authoring wasn't supposed to be like this. I knew full
well that I would be in "start-up mode" during the first
two years as I worked to establish myself in the world
of Christian publishing. But I expected that if I survived
those early days, I would have managed to develop some

semblance of financial and career stability by year three. I was wrong. Everything I had been working to create in my professional life now seemed to be in peril.

In stark contrast, things were thriving on the home front. My boys were maturing in their faith. They were also growing closer together as brothers—bickering less and less and hanging out together more and more. My marriage had never been stronger. Kim and I were working through all of the uncertainty with a remarkable unity. *I'm living a truly blessed life*, I thought to myself when I thought about my family.

Reality would set in, however, when I'd check my empty email inbox or look inside my wallet. Sales of my existing books were flat. A manuscript I had completed nearly six months earlier was still without a contract. I did have two new promising proposals under consideration, but the constant delays from the publisher were discouraging. It got worse. By now, the two long years of start-up mode had taken their toll on our financial resources. To top it off, within weeks of each other, we experienced two car breakdowns, a hard-drive crash on my laptop, and the lowest blow of all for two Java lovers, a broken coffee-maker. *Just in time*, Kim and I would say to each other in times past when God provided for us at the last moment. But now we wondered whether it was going to be replaced by another operative phrase: *Not in time*.

Blessings at home. Near failure at work. As I continued my afternoon run, I began questioning God as I prayed along the way. When I got to my normal turnaround point on the road, I kept on running. I could not stop. A physical challenge was all I wanted at that moment. It was the one activity I could do in my life that could be achieved by sheer willpower.

Frustrated. Confused. Perhaps more so than I had ever been before in my Christian life. But I remained firmly committed to everything we had started. God's call hadn't changed, I reminded myself. I was now wondering, however, if we would be able to survive the summit attempt or whether we were destined to die on the way up.

INTO THIN AIR

When you climb above 26,000 feet on Mount Everest, you enter high altitudes that are known in mountaineering circles as the Death Zone. The oxygen content in the air inside the Death Zone is one-third of what a person can breathe at sea level. In fact, the air is so thin that it cannot sustain human life.

At lower elevations on Everest, the more time a climber trains and acclimatizes, the better his body responds as he travels higher. But the human body is simply incapable of acclimatizing above 26,000 feet. No matter the training. No matter the technology. No matter how much supplemental oxygen he takes along. The body of even an elite climber will begin to shut down if he stays in the Death Zone for any extended period of time. As climbing expert Dave Carter says, "Your mind and body deteriorate within hours. Your brain cells die. Your blood begins to turn to sludge."

When you lack oxygen in the Death Zone, you can become confused and start to make severe errors in judgment. To make matters worse, you can delude yourself into believing you are in complete control and making clear decisions even though you are not. At high altitudes, you also risk developing edema, a circulatory condition that occurs when the body tries to compensate from the lack of oxygen by increasing the blood flow to the brain or lungs.

The Death Zone symbolizes to me the dangers that a man can fall into when he attempts to live as an Expeditionary Man. He is going smack against the culture of our society and even of the church when he launches out with his family in a life of risky, adventurous faith. After all, if he is going to prioritize his family over the office, there can be a deep career or financial cost that accompanies that decision. For some men, the net impact may be relatively minor. But for others, the adjustment is more radical. A man will probably feel exhilaration at the start of this new journey. But as time goes on and the trail grows steeper and the air thinner, he can wonder how he is going to possibly make it through this "Death Zone" and survive the ordeal.

TREKKING INTO THE DEATH ZONE

What does it mean, practically speaking, to live as a modern-day disciple? I've been fascinated, almost fixated, by this question for years. Jesus commands his followers to deny themselves, take up their cross, and follow him (Matt. 16:24). But what does it really mean to "deny yourself" and "take up your cross" in this day and age?

I have often posed that question to my friends, but I am not sure if I have ever heard an answer that fully taps into the edgy nature of Christ's call. Clearly, Jesus is calling his followers to something far beyond *being good, being involved at church,* or *being responsible at home.* That's child's play in his eyes; any run-of-the-mill Pharisee can do that. Instead, he is calling believers to something more: to lose their claim to themselves. "When a man comes to Jesus," Oswald Chambers said, "it is not sin that is in the way, but his claim to himself." What Chambers is driving at is that even after you become a believer, you still want a say on your own life. You want to live the way you want to.

But Dietrich Bonhoeffer brings us back to the fact that I can't keep what's mine and follow him. He says, "When Jesus calls a man, he bids him 'come and die.'" Jesus Christ wants every part of you if you are going to follow him. He wants your family, career, ministry, and hobbies, so that you can be totally loyal to him. Therefore, if a man is going to follow the spirit of Matthew 16:24, this decision will have major implications in his life.

Some men respond to Christ's challenge by entering the ministry or becoming a foreign missionary. They sacrifice a more comfortable lifestyle, financial security, or perhaps a vocation they love to reach the world for Christ. These guys exude discipleship—it's easy to see how Christ's command applies to their lives. But what about other men? How do they "abandon it all" in a culture where nearly everyone has everything they need, if not want? The vast majority of Christians are not called into full-time ministry. We work in the secular world and live a lifestyle comparable to our unbelieving neighbors. Discipleship, in this context, is either lip service for "what we do anyway" or a deliberate decision to *actually* turn over our careers, ministry, and home to Jesus Christ and have the faith to trust God with the results.

When I left the corporate world, my career was the first thing I surrendered to Christ. But as I have already shared, it was not long before I realized that God's calling was broader in scope than just my profession. I got various reactions from other men when I made this move. Some were encouraging, while others were more skeptical. *Rich, you're thirty-seven, is that the right time for putting the brakes on your career? Have you seen how bad the economy is?*

Yet, in spite of the occasional skepticism, I was inspired by those two heroes of mine, evangelist George Müller and missionary Hudson Taylor. Like Müller and Taylor, I wanted to live my new, unchartered life as a modern-day disciple — serve God through my calling as an Expeditionary Man and trust him for the results.

GOD'S TESTING POINTS

During the first two years of my new career, I found myself surviving, more or less, by the seat of my pants while I worked to build a foundation for the future. However, every time things would get tight for us, God always seemed to provide — in typical Müller-esque fashion — at the last possible moment. Our mortgage was due during one of those crunch times, and we received an unexpected check in the mail to cover our shortfall. Our lawnmower broke down, only to have a friend give us their old one. Ominous sounds from the transmission of our aging van seemed to miraculously disappear before we laid down a thousand dollars to fix it. This new life was harder than I ever expected. But because my faith was being refined on an almost daily basis, I discovered I was experiencing more joy than ever before.

"What do we tell the boys?" Kim and I asked each other as money started getting tighter as time went on. My gut reaction was to act like The Protector — shielding them from any uncertainty about finances. As my wife and I discussed the matter further, however, we both became convinced that the opposite response was called for in our situation. In fact, these were *exactly* the sort of issues we should be praying about together as a family. Since God was building the faith of Kim and me, we needed to use this as an opportunity to strengthen the boys' faith at the same time. I did not want them to simply hear about God's blessings after the tension was over.

It's amazing how the Holy Spirit continually reveals new truth to believers through Scripture. In years past, I read Psalm 40 and thought of it as a rather ordinary psalm of worship. However, in my devotions during this time, I found myself drawn deeper and deeper into it. The juxtaposition of gratitude, hope, and desperation in the psalm mirrored the ups and downs I was experiencing in my life. "I waited patiently for the LORD; he turned to me and heard my cry … he set my feet on a rock and gave me a firm place to stand," writes David in the first two verses. The "rock" David is writing about is obviously God himself.

A rock is a common symbol used throughout Scripture to refer to the steadfastness and dependability of God. "The LORD is my rock, my fortress and my deliverer; my God is my rock, in whom I take refuge," says David in Psalm 18:2. He adds later in verse 31, "Who is the Rock except our God?" Jesus Christ is also described by Paul as "the spiritual rock" (1 Cor. 10:4). In 2 Timothy 4:18 the apostle sums it up: "The Lord will rescue me from every evil attack and will bring me safely to his heavenly kingdom."

With these bold promises of Scripture in my pocket, I pressed forward with confidence. When my first book was released early in the second year, I had high hopes that I was finally gaining a foothold in this new world

I was working in. Little did I know the plot was only thickening.

I soon received a verbal "green light" to begin working on a second book. In good faith, I kept busy over the next six months writing the manuscript, but by the end of this time, a last-minute snag beyond the control of my publisher developed, and the whole project got shelved.

Since I'd been working for months without getting paid, I took on side projects to help bridge the income gap. But I was discouraged at the sudden downturn just when momentum seemed to be building. I constantly reminded myself that God was in control. The Scriptures, after all, consistently paint a picture of God closely watching over the nitty-gritty details of our lives. Proverbs tells us that God determines our steps (Prov. 16:9), while Acts says that he arranges the time and places in which we live (Acts 17:26).

"God engineers circumstances" is one of the common sayings of Oswald Chambers. In fact, his writings were so meaningful to me at this time that I typed up a page of his quotes that I'd read through during times of doubt. Listen to Chambers:

- When once the saint begins to realize that God engineers circumstances, there will be no more whine, but only a reckless abandon to Jesus.

- God engineers our circumstances as He did those of His Son; all we have to do is to follow where He places us. The majority of us are busy trying to place ourselves. God alters things while we wait for Him.

- We have an idea that we have to alter things, we have not; we have to remain true to God in the midst of things as they are, to allow things as they are to transmute us.

Looking back, I think God was probably "acclimatizing" my family during the first two years as we went through a series of mini-crises followed by clear responses from him. He seemed to be giving us these small tests of faith to toughen us up for what we'd face in that third year: our version of the Death Zone.

As my third-year anniversary was approaching, our situation became even more challenging. When I brainstormed more and prayed less, common sense would lead me to taking decisive action. *Rich, do something, anything!* So I toyed with selling our house and moving to a cheaper part of the country and continuing on. I considered getting a "real job" and putting my writing career on hold until sales picked up on my books. But when I prayed and fasted and sought counsel from my pastor and other close friends, I came to the opposite conclusion. I found God consistently bringing me back to the same place: *stay on course for the time being; at this particular place, God wants us to do what we are doing.*

I found that same message coming through loudly in Psalm 40. After all, it is a psalm that must be read with patient lips. "I waited patiently for the LORD," writes David at the beginning. God never promises that he will immediately wave his magic wand and deliver us from the pit. On the contrary, David conveys the sense that his rescue, while certain, was a long time in coming. So I pressed on, remaining steadfast in the midst of uncertainty. My peace and trust is evident in an email I sent to a friend during this period of my life:

The good news (actually great news) is that I have

such a major peace about our whole situation. I've not been anxious or panicked about the situation at all over the past few weeks, even though it is certainly the most [challenging] in the 18 years that we've been married. I really believe we are where God wants us right now, and believe we are being faithful in living out what he wants us to do. I have no other choice than to trust that he will lead us and guide us.

Yet, as we continued to struggle, the faith stories of Müller and Taylor began to feel like a tease to me. The biographical accounts of their lives seemed to paint an overly pristine, sanitized portrait of what discipleship is—that with enough faith and prayer, God will always provide for the needs of a believer just in time. I wondered, *Didn't Müller and Taylor ever struggle with times of doubt and uncertainty? Did they ever feel like God abandoned them?*

Müller and Taylor had become examples of a faith that was either unrealistic or unattainable by a mere mortal like me. I had this image of the two of them taking a climb through the high altitudes of Everest. But instead of struggling and hanging on for dear life, angels were marking the trails, fixing rope, supplying supplemental oxygen, and clearing the obstacles for them all the way to the top.

But if Müller and Taylor seemed harder to relate to than ever, I found myself identifying more and more with the David of the psalms, whose faith was shaped, refined, molded, battle-hardened, and perfected through adversity and testing. I had a second image in my mind, this one in which David is climbing up Everest and struggling every step of the way in the Death Zone. A storm is raging around him. With visibility almost zero, David stumbles on a boulder of ice and falls headfirst into the snow. As he works to catch his breath, David cries out for help to God in desperation—but sees no angels to help him out. For a moment, he considers just giving up. He could, after all, just lie down and freeze to death in a matter of minutes. But shaking off those feelings of futility, David suddenly rises to his feet, shakes off the snow, and continues upward in faith.

I am now a year removed from that testing period of my life. Circumstances have stabilized somewhat, and we've not been in crisis mode for a while. But times are still uncertain. I see my boys getting older, and I know the challenges around the corner for paying for their college tuition. *Tick tock.* And I am realistic enough to know that a full-time writer can only be in start-up mode for so long and still attract publishers. *Tick tock.* I continue in faith, but I still have bouts of doubt. I find myself identifying with the candor of Mark 9:24: "I do believe; help me overcome my unbelief!" That verse effectively sums up the split personality of my faith.

Yet, in spite of these constant challenges and unknowns over the past five years, I would not change a thing. I've come to realize that his blessings are far more than professional and financial. I find it impossible to deny the transforming work that he continues to do inside us.

Topping it off, I have come to see that our struggles, in and of themselves, have actually been blessings. Not only did hard times bring us closer together as a family, but they also taught the boys character, patience, and a gratefulness that they never had before.

There is a memorable scene in *Elizabethtown* in which the main character, Drew Baylor, is fired from a giant athletic shoe company after his design gaffe costs the company nearly a billion dollars. Reflecting on his situation, Drew says, "No true fiasco ever began as a quest for mere adequacy. A motto of the British Special Air Force is: 'Those who risk, win.' A single green vine shoot is able to grow through cement. The Pacific Northwestern salmon beats itself bloody on its quest to travel hundreds of miles upstream against the current, with a single purpose ... life." I often find myself wondering whether, in the end, this life of godly adventure I am pursuing will turn out to be a "true fiasco." But I am comforted that I am striving for much more than "mere adequacy" as a disciple, husband, father, and a man.

A COMMUNIQUÉ FROM THE DEATH ZONE

During rough weather on Everest, an expedition will often send two expert climbers or Sherpas ahead to set snow poles, fix rope, or check out the snow and ice. This advance team will be in regular radio contact back to the leader, informing everyone of the route and weather conditions. This sort of advance information is critical to the decisions being made for the team as a whole on the ascent.

Over the past few years, I have spent more time than what I'd like in a Death Zone. In the process, I have received some "advance information" that has made me far more realistic about what it means to live as an Expeditionary Man in a fallen, imperfect world.

To begin, I am convinced that the commitment to live by faith will inevitably lead a man through God's testing grounds—his Death Zone, so to speak. James 1:3 tells us flat out that God will test our faith to produce endurance.

Given that truth, everything I have experienced—doubt, isolation, and frustration—really should have been expected all along. I should have been more realistic that such testing can be far messier and grittier than I planned for. After all, let me return to Mount Everest for a moment. With the mountain's one-in-ten casualty rate, there are obviously no guaranteed formulas for success. Risk and danger is a part of every climb, no matter how well prepared, supplied, equipped, or experienced the climbing team is.

In addition, I've come to realize that living by faith is not a simple matter of cause and effect. In the past, I wonder if I looked on my decision to live a life of risky faith as a sort of gentlemen's agreement between God and myself. It went something like this: I will serve God in whatever profession he calls me and devote myself to leading and discipling my family. He, in turn, will take care of us.

I hear this message all the time from pulpits. *If you tithe, then you will be blessed. If you trust, he will provide. If you do X, then he will do Y.* Christ does promise that he will provide, answer our prayers, and give to us what we need. But his response is not always so cut and dried. My journey has shown me that we can't constrain God to a simple cause-and-effect plan. The call to discipleship, after all, is anything but a gentlemen's agreement. It's an invitation to "come and die." Period. End of story. There are no conditions, says Christ, if you want to follow me (Matt. 8:18–22).

Political scientists commonly used a term to describe Cold War era politics: *Realpolitik. Realpolitik* is a German expression that means the "politics of reality," a foreign policy based on practical concerns rather than getting bogged down in debates about theory. Perhaps believers should come up with a similar term, *Realglaube* (meaning "real faith"), as an honest way to describe how faith plays out in our humanness. A gritty *Realglaube* contrasts with a Teflon-coated, smiley-faced faith that is often lauded in churches but rarely lived out consistently in our lives. As David illustrates throughout the Psalms, we live in a state of *Realglaube*, a constant tension between our spiritual hope in God's deliverance and the stark reality that it doesn't always come as we expect it to.

LESSON NUMBER 3

Perhaps you saw the 1998 film *Ronin*, a spy thriller that tells the story of former Cold War intelligence agents on a mission to retrieve a mysterious briefcase. Vincent, an ex-French spy, is in charge of the logistics of the Paris-based operation. Even after Vincent risks his life several times during the course of the movie to successfully obtain the case, the people who hired him take it from him before he ever discovers its contents. In the closing lines of the film, Vincent reflects on living in a world where he fails to see much resolution on the work that he performs: "No questions. No answers. That's the business we're in. You just accept it and move on. Maybe that's lesson number three."

Vincent touches on a key truth for men and all believers in his "lesson number three." Perhaps this truth gets to the heart of what it means to live as a modern-day disciple: *live for Christ with such a steadfast faith that we need no explanations when life doesn't go as planned.*

For a brief time last year, I wondered how I could possibly write this book, encouraging other men to shake up their livelihoods for the sake of their families. After all,

I sometimes felt as if God had left me for dead in the Death Zone. Why should I subject others to a similar death march? However, I came to realize that the very fact that things did not always go smoothly for me is *exactly* why I needed to write the book. If God had made the path easy, I imagine that my perspective would have been as the expert with everything figured out. I would have had my own "cookie cutter" formula that a man simply needed to follow to navigate the Death Zone en route to the summit.

But here I offer no formulas or blueprints. I simply encourage every Christian man to surrender his claim to his life, be directed by the Holy Spirit, seek wise counsel from godly men, be accountable to others, and persevere no matter what happens.

During the early bleak days of World War II, several British soldiers and spies were trying to escape France and Holland and return to the British Isles. In order to communicate over radio to England and avoid German interception, they used a seemingly harmless phrase as the password: "But if not." While the phrase may have seemed benign, the underlying message was powerful. The soldiers were referencing a line from the King James Version of the book of Daniel (3:18). In this passage, Shadrach, Meshach, and Abednego were getting ready to be sent to a fiery furnace as a punishment for not bowing to King Nebuchadnezzar. Before the execution is carried out, Shadrach offers a final message to the king, "We expect God to save the day, but if not, we will still serve him." From their secret message, the British soldiers were telling England that they hoped they'd be rescued, but if not, they would not succumb to the Nazis, even if it cost them their lives.

"But if not" has become a climbing mantra for me and my family. I expect God will protect and provide for us as we walk through the Death Zone. But if not, we will still walk in faith toward the summit until we can walk, crawl, and breathe no more. Until then, farther up, farther in.

NOW TO THE SUMMIT

In my quest for biblical manhood, I have mapped the course, laid the ropes, and marked the mountain trail. Now it's time to climb to the summit, attacking the mountain with a "siege strategy" like the great Everesters of old. With a commitment to Jesus Christ as the starting point, a man climbs upward to essential milestones along the way. In Camp 1, a man pauses his career; in Camp 2, he limits his church ministries. A man makes an investment in his children's education in Camp 3 and disciples his family in Camp 4. Each of these four commitments is a critical stepping stone to the overall summit attempt. Camps 1 and 2 reorient a man's heart for adventure and enable him to be successful at Camps 3 and 4.

On an Everest climb, climbers move up to different camps and back down over successive weeks to acclimatize to the higher altitudes. That process mirrors the experience of a committed man. He does not just go from one camp to the next, checking them off like checkboxes on a to-do list. Instead, during the process of becoming the man God wants him to be, he gradually "acclimatizes" his heart, allowing Christ to reorient all of these major areas of manhood in accordance with his will.

Every mountain climb begins with an initial footstep. And for one intent on becoming an Expeditionary Man, that first step must be his career. For most of us, giving our career fully to Jesus Christ is going to be the most difficult stride of all. When I finally took this step in my life, little did I know I would soon be doing things that I never would have imagined.

PART 3

BECOMING AN EXPEDITIONARY MAN

Find a way or make one.
—Frank Hurley, *Shackleton*

No one who has ever lived a life of ease
has lived a life worth living.
—Jay Kesler, former president
of Youth for Christ

You are my greatest adventure,
and I almost missed it.
—Mr. Incredible to his family,
The Incredibles

CHAPTER 9

CAMP #1: PAUSING YOUR CAREER

We both worked so hard and ... for what?
We should have taken this trip years ago.
— Drew Baylor (to an urn containing
his father's ashes), *Elizabethtown*

It's Monday morning, 9:00 a.m. The to-do list on my whiteboard is filled with items I must get through today. My monitor and computer are on and ready to go. The cursor in Microsoft Word is blinking, waiting for human input. But my office is empty and my chair is unoccupied. At this time of the day, you will find me by walking through the kitchen, past the family room, and then going up a side stairway to a room above our garage. I am up here each weekday morning teaching my boys history, literature, and logic over the next couple of hours. It will not be until lunchtime that I am free to start tackling that to-do list.

During the prime time of a normal workday, my career is now taking a backseat spot, both on my calendar and in my heart. This life change would be quite startling for anyone who knew me a decade ago. My motif at that time was to dash out of bed at the crack of dawn and speed off to the office to get a jumpstart on the workday. I looked forward to Monday mornings the way others do to TGIF.

Today, when deadlines loom and work piles up, this arrangement is, quite candidly, a struggle. My productivity suffers, especially when I swap my morning work time with the late-night shift and usually am forced to get by with little sleep. I also am realistic enough to know that I am making it harder on myself to meet deadlines and am leaving opportunities on the table that I simply cannot get to. But in spite of these limitations, I remain fully committed to this godly adventure that God has called me to. After all, my calling as a disciple is not so much to be a Christian author as it is to be an Expeditionary Man.

If a man is going to be a hands-on leader to his family, the first and often greatest challenge he has to overcome is surrendering his career aspirations when his children are living at home. Jesus Christ is not going to call all men to homeschool their kids or work the midnight shift. But he is looking for every man to increase his devotion to his family and decrease his dedication to his work. For some men, this commitment will mean foregoing a lucrative promotion or opportunity.

For others, it will entail placing strict limits on the amount of business travel or work hours they are willing to do in order to minimize TAFF, or Time Away From Family. (I capitalize the term "Time Away From Family" simply to identify it as a real, legitimate opponent rather than letting it slip through unnamed under the radar.) For telecommuters and men with more flexible schedules, this commitment will prompt them to shift their workday around so that they can be more of an active presence in their families. Finally, for a handful, it will mean giving up a career that proves itself to be incompatible with living out a godly adventure at home.

Working men generally fall into one of four career categories. Each of these categories has its own opportunities, challenges, and pressure points for becoming an Expeditionary Man.

- The *Officemates* are in professions (such as a doctor, construction worker, or factory supervisor) that require a man to be at the office, factory, or place of employment all the time. As a result, minimizing TAFF is the continual ground-zero battleground.

- The *Hybrids* are men who telecommute one or more days a week. Telecommuting provides a significant opportunity for men to work hard for their employer while at the same time immersing themselves more and more on the home front.

- The *Homesteaders* are men who work at home all the time and perhaps even partner with their wives to homeschool their kids. Their lifestyle is almost a throwback to an earlier era and offers the chance to have an essential unity of purpose across a man's vocation, his wife's role in the household, and his children's education.

- Finally, the *Survivormen* are men who are simply struggling to survive. A Survivorman is at or near the poverty level and risks being on the street if he cannot pull in two or more jobs. Obviously, in this desperate situation, a man really has to do the best that he can to provide for his family—all the while praying constantly that the Lord gives him the opportunity to play a hands-on leadership role in his family. But, during those precious moments when he is at home, he must rely on the Holy Spirit to grant him the energy needed to invest himself in his children.

Becoming an Expeditionary Man is not about what a man does in his profession. Nor is it about the location of his work place. I discovered the adventure of leading my family as I began working at home. But that is my own individual experience and not something that every man is going to be called by Jesus Christ to do. Instead, becoming an Expeditionary Man is all about a transformation of a man's heart, whether he is a doctor working at a hospital, pastor at a church, bus driver on the road, or a real estate agent working out of his home.

More Than Just a Worker Bee

My house is about ninety minutes outside of Boston, and though I enjoy jogging, I pay no attention to professional track-and-field sports. However, every April, anyone living in New England knows that you cannot help but hear about long-distance running during the annual Boston Marathon. Over the past two decades, African athletes have gained the reputation for being the fastest long-distance runners in the world and fully dominate this prestigious race. In fact, it has been nearly thirty years since an American has won the event.

Suppose, for a moment, there is a Boston-native amateur—he's fictional, so let's call him Desmond—who starts dominating every local race he runs in. As his victories mount, the press begins to portray Desmond as a local folk hero, the great upstart. Not surprisingly, when the Boston Marathon comes around the following spring, locals are convinced that Desmond has a legitimate shot at winning the race and rallies around him.

Race day comes and the marathon begins. Desmond initially holds up well against the competition. After twenty miles, he is actually running neck and neck in the lead with a Kenyan and a South African runner. However, watching the race from the finish line on a large television monitor, a large crowd suddenly notices that Desmond is nowhere in sight of the two leaders at mile marker 21. *What happened?* the crowd murmurs. One minute passes, then two. People in the crowd are speculating. *He injured his leg*, says one man. Another counters, *No, he gave up and went home.* After several more anxious moments, the local favorite is seen again back on the race course, running all-out in an effort to move back into contention with the two African runners. In the end, Desmond is able to close the gap slightly, but eventually finishes a distant third.

After the race, the crowd and the media is clamoring to know why he went MIA for those 120 seconds. Some are upset, while others are plain confused. *How could a competitive marathon runner take time out of his race? It doesn't make any sense at all.* However, perceptions change once the local reporters interview several eyewitnesses to what had happened earlier in the day. Bystanders along the route report that just as Desmond was passing a crowd of spectators at the 20.5 mile mark, an elderly onlooker fainted beside the road in an apparent heat stroke. Being a medical resident, Desmond immediately stopped to help treat the man and make sure he was okay before continuing on.

Realizing the motivation for his actions, his fans quickly forget about the race. Desmond's response is not only justified, but also the only right thing he could have done in that situation. As a result, Desmond emerges as more than a great athlete in the eyes of his fans; he is now a full-fledged hero.

When a man pauses his career ambitions, others who define him in terms of his profession will probably respond much like Desmond's fans initially did. *How could he do that?* After all, the idea of a man voluntarily diverting his energy and pulling himself out of the "career game," even if only temporarily, goes against the competitive nature of our economy. People want a man to be devoted at home, but the notion of a man sacrificing his career and God-given abilities is hard for most to grasp.

Balance is a malleable word, a term that a man can mold into most anything that he wants. *Pause,* on the other hand, is far more rigid. There is just no way around its all-or-nothing nature. Something is either paused or it isn't. I am reminded of an evening several months ago that was not one of my finer moments. I was relaxing on the couch watching a DVD while Kim was baking in the kitchen. Across the room, she began talking with me about an issue she was having at work. I was already engrossed in the film, so my gut reaction was to multitask—listening to her while I continued to watch the movie.

You can guess what happened next. As the movie plot got more and more absorbing, I began nodding and trying to inject phrases like *Really?... Um hum ... Ah, yes* during her pauses. Kim soon saw what was happening, so she began making up a bizarre story to see if I was listening *... And then I got mugged by Superman on the way out to the parking garage. And then ...* Upon hearing "mugging" and

"Superman" in the same sentence, I knew I was busted. I immediately hit the Pause button on my remote, realizing that such a response was the only "Expeditionary-Man-thing-to-do" to salvage this awkward moment. With the movie no longer being a distraction, I could now give her my full attention. Kim and I laugh about that incident, but it does make clear the inherent differences between "balancing" and "pausing."

The Bible is clear on the need to work (Eph. 4:28; 1 Thess. 5:14; 2 Thess. 3:12), but not overly specific on the subject of career advancement. As a result, it is easy for a Christian man to start with the presuppositions of our culture and economy, add in a strong work ethic, and then shape a biblical response on top of that foundation. But when he does so, the idea of pausing his career strikes an ill chord. It sounds half-baked and irresponsible, against what makes a man a man. Capitalism, after all, teaches that the hardest, most committed workers will reap the rewards. The Protestant work ethic follows suit, teaching that a man is to work his hardest in everything he does to bring God glory.

Obviously, a man is called to glorify God and to be dedicated to his job, but that does not mean that all career decisions should be measured against the rules of the modern economy. As the story of Desmond illustrates, a man is more than just a worker bee. As such, there is a broader context in which a Christian man makes such give-and-take decisions.

CHRIST SENSE

Derek is a successful businessman and father of two. If you were to meet him at church, you would consider him a friendly, even gregarious man. But in spite of his easygoing demeanor, he is a shark at work and can tear through business deals with a mixture of shrewdness and skill. Derek and I shared a common bond at a critical decision point in our lives. You know about my leap-of-faith career story already. Well, Derek was less sure of what exactly he was praying for, but he knew he was dissatisfied with the status quo. He sensed time was running out with his children and wanted to make a life change to minimize TAFF. He was financially well off, certainly positioned to make a career transition without experiencing any pinch for quite some time. But when I talked with him, he seemed paralyzed from being able to seriously consider any action. In reading between the lines, I could sense Derek thinking to himself, "Men in my position don't switch their vocations just because they don't get enough time with their families ... it's totally impractical."

Derek's struggle was not against inner ambition or drive, but against common sense. Common sense holds that a man like Derek play it safe, provide for his family, and let his "better half" focus on the kids. Many believers, in fact, see common sense as God's wisdom for practical living. Kim received an email the other day that expressed this mind-set. In the letter, the writer stated, "God's Word is clear that we should use our minds, so it's fine for us to use common sense to make decisions."

This writer's logic certainly sounds good and reasonable. After all, common sense is a gift that God gives to us as a guide and barometer for responsible Christian living. But we have to be careful with it, because common sense can also lead us astray. In fact, the more I study the Scriptures, the more I see how easy it is for common sense to become an archenemy to genuine faith. The apostle Paul contrasts the common-sense wisdom of the world and the word of Jesus Christ in 1 Corinthians 3:18–20:

> If any one of you think you are wise by the standards of this age, you should become "fools" so that you may become wise. For the wisdom of this world is foolishness in God's sight. As it is written: "He catches the wise in their craftiness"; and again, "The Lord knows that the thoughts of the wise are futile."

Additionally, while the book of Proverbs is filled with "common sense" adages, it underscores the need to put trust and obedience above all else (Prov. 3:5–7, emphasis mine):

> Trust in the LORD with all your heart,
>   and *lean not on your own understanding*;
> in all your ways submit to him,
>   and he will make your paths straight.
> *Do not be wise in your own eyes*;
>   fear the LORD and shun evil.

Leaning on our own understanding is something easier said than done, however. Oswald Chambers explains, "The majority of us do not enthrone God, we enthrone common sense. We make our decisions and then ask the real God to bless our god's decision ... Common sense is not faith, and faith is not common sense."

One of the subtle underlying themes throughout Scripture is a contrast between common sense and what I call "Christ sense," or a faith-inspired wisdom. In fact, I wonder if there is a faithful follower of God written about in the Bible who led a risk-averse, safe life. Consider Noah. He spent 120 years of his life building an ark, an activity that was sheer lunacy to the world around him. Moses abandoned common sense and a life of wealth and power when he identified himself as an Israelite rather than stay inside his royal Egyptian cocoon.

Fast forward to the time just before the Israelites were preparing to cross the Jordan River. The tribes of Reuben and Gad, well known for their large herds and flocks, were content to stay put east of the Jordan rather than go forward with the others into the Promised Land. "Do not make us cross the Jordan," they pleaded to Moses and the other leaders (Num. 32:5). Moses was not pleased by the request. He felt it showed a lack of faith and an unwillingness to risk their well-being for the sake of following the Lord. In the end, the account of this story in Numbers 32 reads like a face-off between a group motivated by common sense (Reubenites and Gadites) and another group led by Christ sense (Moses, Joshua, and the rest of the Israelites).

Centuries later, Gideon led Israel to victory against the Midianites. Yet common sense among the Israelites of the day would have held him to be the least likely man to lead their nation into a war. After all, he was in the weakest clan in the tribe of Manasseh and was the least inside of his family.

Skip ahead to David. When the prophet Samuel chose the successor to Saul, he traveled to the house of Jesse. Common sense dictated selecting one of David's more physically striking and charismatic brothers. Instead, Samuel selected the youngest and least impressive of them all, David.

I'll jump ahead to Jesus Christ during his earthly ministry. Everything about him defied the common wisdom of his day. He didn't look the part of a Messiah; he was not particularly attractive, dynamic, or hypnotic to listen to

(Isa. 53:2). He came from Nazareth, the last place people expected the Messiah to come from (John 1:46). Jesus picked uneducated fishermen, tax collectors, and other commoners to establish his church, not an elite group of talented leaders. Finally, he came to bring spiritual salvation rather than the political revolt that the Jewish masses expected from the Messiah of Israel. Oswald Chambers sums up his ministry, saying "Nothing Jesus Christ ever said is common sense."

Perhaps nowhere in Scripture does the tension between faith and common sense play out more comprehensively than in Abraham's life. Abraham had several tests in which he had to decide whether or not he was going to live by faith. He starts out strong in Genesis 12 when God asks him to leave his homeland and go in faith to the land of Canaan. *Round 1, faith.*

But Abram (Abraham) backslides once he gets there. When a severe famine hits the region, he is forced to travel with his wife Sarai (Sarah) to Egypt for food. However, because Sarah is so physically attractive, Abraham grows convinced that they will encounter an Egyptian who will kill him so that he can take Sarah for his own. Rather than trusting that God will deliver them safely, he comes up with his own scheme of protection—lie about it. So, when the pressure is turned on, Abraham tells the Pharaoh's officials that Sarah is his sister. *Round 2, common sense.*

Years later (Gen. 16), Abraham struggles with the reality that even though God has promised him an heir, he still has no son. And with his barren wife Sarah becoming quite old, he grows more and more desperate. Once again, Abraham can choose whether to remain patient and trust in God for a miracle or else seek to manufacture an alternative solution. When he hears Sarah's plan—to sleep with her maidservant Hagar—the idea clicks, so he follows through with it. *Round 3, common sense.*

In both of these major tests of faith, Abraham's actions can be justified from an earthly perspective. He is, after all, only trying to achieve a desired result through the resources and knowledge that are available to him at the time. But looking back today, we can see that his actions lead to only negative complications. The Egyptian pharaoh and his household are struck with severe diseases because he took Sarah in. Abraham and Sarah are eventually expelled from the country once the pharaoh learns of his lie. So too, Hagar's birth of Ishmael causes conflict and strife in the lives of Abraham, his son Isaac, and their descendants.

Finally, God offers the toughest test of faith for Abraham in Genesis 22. Abraham is instructed to go to the land of Moriah and offer his son Isaac up as a burnt offering to the Lord. Once again, Abraham has a choice. He can rationalize and take a common-sense approach: *God promised me that I would be the father of many nations. So, when he tells me to sacrifice Isaac, he must be really saying that I should symbolically sacrifice him when I really offer a lamb as burnt offering instead.* But this time Abraham will have none of it. He knows he has no other choice but to go against common sense and simply obey, trusting that God knows what he is doing. *Final round, faith (KO).*

In the past, when reading Genesis 22, I considered God's testing of Abraham in Moriah as bordering on being extreme, almost cruel. But as I began to look at the situation in light of an earlier life often dominated by common-sense decisions, I realized that God was forced to do whatever it took to get Abraham to live by faith. If he had consistently trusted God as he did when he left for Canaan, I wonder whether he would have had to go through such heartbreaking testing on Mount Moriah.

In the end, Abraham chose to trust in God and is now one of the pillars of faith highlighted in Hebrews 11. He learned that following God's call involves single-minded obedience, not a pragmatic interpretation of how that call should be fulfilled.

A STUMBLING BLOCK

A man's decision to put his family over his career is not necessarily guaranteed to be a popular decision inside the walls of his home. It's a tough enough choice for a man, but it may be even more difficult for his wife and family. Sometimes the desire for security drowns out the benefits of having a more committed husband or father.

Remember the scene in *Field of Dreams* in which Ray Kinsella hears The Voice a second time when it tells him to "Ease his pain." Ray ends up becoming convinced that The Voice is calling him to go to Boston to bring reclusive author Terence Mann back with him to Iowa. Ray's wife, Anni, who was initially supportive of Ray building the baseball field, now wants nothing more of this "voice business." She is far more concerned about the strain that the baseball field has placed on them financially and the possibility of losing the farm.

Ray sticks to his beliefs and Anni is ultimately convinced that he should continue in his quest, but I am struck by the squandering that would have occurred had Ray stopped at this point and given into Anni. None of the larger plan would have been accomplished. Ray's purpose, after all, was not just to build a field for Shoeless

Joe; instead, that act was merely the catalyst for something far greater and life-changing for Ray and his family—reconciliation with Ray's father.

Likewise, a man's wife, a relative, or a close friend can be well meaning as they argue against him pausing his career. In doing so, they can became a major temptation for him to put the brakes on doing anything that goes against what is safest and most secure for his loved ones. Perhaps the best illustration comes from Jesus himself when Peter argues over the fact of whether Jesus would be killed (Matt. 16:21–23). Jesus responds strongly to Peter, saying, "Get behind me, Satan! You are a stumbling block to me." Jesus may sound harsh, but only until we understand the context. He fully recognized that Satan was tempting him in one of his most vulnerable places—by using one of his closest disciples as his principal means of temptation.

Pausing a career has the potential for being a divisive issue for a husband and wife and, therefore, should be done only through studying God's Word, praying and fasting together, seeking godly counsel, and both having a sincere desire to live in faith. In the end, the decision needs to be a unifying factor in a marriage, not a disruptive one.

As I have already shared, I first paused my career years ago by staying in a dead-end job. I did so because the job was "family friendly," allowing me to work at home for much of the week. While the decision was made self-sacrificially, the problem was that I did not follow it up with any renewed focus on the home front. And since I was still expecting to find adventure and purpose in my vocation, I ended up finding the whole experience demoralizing, even emasculating. As a result, pausing a career may be the starting point to becoming an Expeditionary Man, but it is insufficient in and of itself. For example, some men will immediately fill the void left by their career with church ministries and let them become a preoccupation. But a ministry offers its own set of risks to the family, as we will soon see.

CHAPTER 10

Camp 2: Limiting Your Ministry

*Ruth says those of us who were traveling missed
the best part our lives — enjoying the children
as they grew. She is probably right.
I was too busy preaching all over the world.*
— Billy Graham

If you have the time...

In an era before YouTube and camcorders, Joe's son, Richie, loved making audiocassette recordings. Some were funny, some were intended to be serious and professional. The most memorable of them all, however, was one that Richie recorded for his dad in which he kept reusing the phrase "If you have the time" over and over and over again. Years later, the phrase became an inside joke for the family. At holidays, Joe would get the tape out from the attic and everyone would sit around the table and listen to it, howling at the high-pitched voice that was trying hard to be oh-so-serious. Yet, underneath the comedy, there was something curious about that phrase. Perhaps there was something more to consider.

Joe was in his mid-thirties with two young children when he was appointed pastor of a struggling suburban church. A key to his decision to enter the ministry a decade earlier was his need to be "sold out" to Jesus Christ. To the young pastor, devoting his life to Christ was not an abstract concept; it meant giving all his time and energy in service to the church. During Joe's tenure, his devotion helped turn the church around and transformed it into a growing, vibrant congregation.

Take a workaholic, an idea guy, a natural-born leader, and a believer who is convinced that he can always do more. Bundle them up into one person and you will have a pastor who becomes involved in every ministry he touches. That was Joe, and it was not long after arriving that he began working with a nearby orphanage and other local ministries in the city. Two years later, he went on his first overseas missions trip to Haiti, an event that changed his life. He began to live and breathe missions. Joe soon headed up district and conference missions programs for his denomination, led over a dozen high school youth missions trips to Haiti, and served as chairman of the board of a nondenominational medical missions program.

Because of his zeal for all-things-ministry, the idea of giving priority to his family never really entered Joe's thought process. To him:

Devotion to Christ = Devotion to church ministry

His family commitment, not surprisingly, had to be subordinate to his church work. As a result, Joe spent his days at church and his evenings involved in missions and other programs. When his son and daughter wanted to play, Joe allotted a set amount of minutes with them before he went back to his den. He justified his TAFF—you know, Time Away From Family—with the belief that the demands of a pastor are different from most vocations. In his mind, he was really never away from his work; there was always one more thing to do. He was called to respond to any given crisis that came up, regardless of what he had planned with his family. "Being involved in ministry placed many demands on my life," Joe says as he looks back today. Then shaking his head, he corrects himself, "No, as a pastor, *I* placed many demands on my life."

Joe's children never complained, so he never even considered making any changes while they were growing up. Yet, as Joe reflects today on this time of his life, he thinks back to that audiotape that his son made. "You know, it never really dawned on me at the time, but perhaps my son was really saying all along, 'I want more of your time, Dad.'"

PUSHING
TOWARD HOME

Joe's mantra went something like this: *If Christ is the Lord of your life, then service to him requires family sacrifice.* Joe is not unique. His perspective on Christian service is common to many committed men involved in ministry, whether they are full-time pastors and missionaries or laymen serving as elders, deacons, Bible study leaders, or church committee members. After all, Jesus says in Matthew 19:29, "And everyone who has left houses or brothers or sisters or father or mother or children or fields for my sake will receive a hundred times as much and will inherit eternal life." And then in Luke 14:26, "If anyone comes to me and does not hate father and mother, wife and children ... such a person cannot be my disciple." They read these passages and take them to mean that they are called to forego their family to reach the world with the gospel.

The downfall with this line of thinking, however, is that it needlessly places a man's family in direct opposition to the service of Christ. Christian service is seen as something that can only take place outside in the world. Serving Christ within the context of a man's family is never even considered a legitimate alternative. But that interpretation takes Jesus' words out of context. Christ is not down on family. No, he is after a man's heart and is adamant that nothing—including a spouse or child—will ever get in the way of devotion to him. What a man does in his life in response to that dedication is a different question altogether.

A few months back, I attended a men's conference on discipleship. Men are to love God, the speaker emphasized, by dying to themselves and living as disciples. So far so good. But it is how he suggested we are to live as disciples that left me feeling uneasy. During the course of the discussion, the speaker began talking about the barriers to faithfulness in the life of a man. In particular, he squared in on the danger of a man's family becoming an idol to him. Quoting Luke 14:26, he confessed that the number one hindrance in his life to loving God was his family. Since his nationwide speaking appearances frequently took him away from his home, he viewed his traveling as a painful but necessary sacrifice he needed to make if he truly loved God.

The speaker clearly had a heart for Christ, but I was struck by his reasoning: why equate traveling around the country with loving God? Can't a man love God just as much by limiting his ministry travels (for a season) so he can devote himself more to his family? Sadly, this dedicated Christian man was so fixated on the command of Jesus to "go into all the world and make disciples" that he was ignoring the blueprint of biblical fatherhood that leaps from the whole body of Scripture. In the end, rather than lumping all married, single, and older men together, shouldn't a more fundamental question be asked: How exactly does a man love God and serve him inside the particular circumstances that he is in?

It is a dangerous thing to tell a sincere believer that his family is the number one threat to loving God. Satan will pick up on that in a heartbeat and run with it. In reality, I am convinced that few men actually struggle with being enslaved by family relationships and treat them as idols. A far more potent danger is a man becoming so devoted to a ministry that he leaves his family behind.

Author Gene Williams urges pastors, "Ministry begins at home, and every minister's primary mission field is his home address." That same principle is applicable to pastors and laymen alike. If a man's family is his primary mission field when his kids are growing up inside his home, he needs to place handcuffs on his church ministry commitments during that period of his life.

The apostle Paul implicitly affirms the idea that a man is first and foremost responsible for family discipleship before his church involvement. After all, in listing qualifications for church leadership, Paul tells Timothy that a man "must manage his own family well and see that his children obey him, and he must do so in a manner worthy of full respect" (1 Tim. 3:4). Notice Paul's order of precedence: a man needs to be successful in his primary mission field *before* extending his ministry to the church.

However, a word of warning. A man who limits his ministry commitments will rarely get a pat on the back from others in his church. Today's Christian culture holds that the more mature you are in your faith, the more active you will be in a ministry. Therefore, when a man is less visible at church, people assume he is either less committed or is backsliding. When I stepped back from leading a Bible study, I had a church leader immediately call me wondering what was going on. "I am not pulling back at all," I said, "but simply *pushing* more of myself toward home."

CHEATING YOURSELF

If you haven't already guessed it, I was the boy named Richie in the story at the beginning of the chapter. *If you have the time* were the words I spoke to my dad on that cassette tape back in 1974. I grew up in a family in which my dad was gone much of the time at church both day and night. I missed him, but accepted it. My sister had a harder time than I did and had occasions where she resented Dad's devotion to the ministry above our family. But her faith survived intact, and she continues to walk in Christ today.

I don't want to paint too dark a picture here. Both of us were impacted in countless ways by my father and his commitment to Christ. Even though we missed him being away much of the time, we at least knew he was doing it for the glory of God and not his own glorification. I recently stumbled across a note I wrote to him when was a teenager. In it I said, "Father, I am proud of you. I feel honored to be called your son." Similarly, my sister looks back today and realizes that the reasons why she went into ministry-oriented positions in her career were largely because of the constructive influence of Dad.

My sister and I avoided becoming statistical victims—those six out of ten Christian kids who leave their faith during their twenties. But there still was a cost to his all-out devotion to the ministry: Dad ended up cheating himself by missing out on many unforgettable experiences with our family.

Believers have eternity to enjoy, but that does not mean we will be able to relive times past on earth. As C. S. Lewis once said, God does not do encores. There are unique blessings associated with this temporal, earthly life that, if missed, are gone forever. A man's kids may dwell with him in eternity, but as the old saying goes, "they are only young once." I think many men who prioritize their ministry over their family will look back someday later in life, or in heaven, and realize they missed out on some important times while their kids were growing up in the home.

In one of the most insightful chapters of his autobiography, *Just As I Am*, Billy Graham talks candidly about the impact his ministry had on his family. The issue was his almost nonstop travel to evangelistic crusades around the world. Throughout the time in which his children were under his roof, his ministry was his focus and passion, even to the exclusion of his family responsibilities. Billy reflects, "Ruth says those of us who were traveling missed the best part our lives—enjoying the children as they grew. She is probably right. I was too busy preaching all over the world."

He continues by considering the cost that his ministry had on both him and his family. "Only Ruth and the children can tell what those extended times of separation meant to them. For myself, as I look back, I now know that I came through those years much the poorer both psychologically and emotionally. I missed so much by not being home to see the children grow and develop. The children must carry scars of those separations too."

Billy now regularly warns young evangelists that he comes in contact with not to make the same mistakes he did. "God's ideal for the home," says Billy, "is to have both the father and the mother available to their children throughout their growing years."

LOOSE HANDCUFFS

An Expeditionary Man ministers first and foremost at home, but that is not the end of the story. A man's family should not be his *exclusive* mission field. Instead, once a man has established a home environment that is unified and growing, then he can carefully and wisely begin to devote time to outside ministries—as long as they don't harm his status as the hands-on leader to his family. Doing so not only enables a man to be faithful in service, but helps demonstrate to his children that there is a larger world around them—that they may be the priority to their parents, but not the sole priority. As a man begins to involve himself in church ministries, he should keep in mind four steps to ensure it does not pull him away from his family.

Time it right. When considering a ministry, the first factor a man needs to be aware of is timing. Our instant-oriented culture can impact his decision making, prompting him to feel pressure to get involved even when his kids are at important stages of growth. But contrast that hastiness with Christ himself. Jesus Christ didn't begin his public ministry as soon as he became an adult. Instead, he waited patiently for over a decade before revealing himself to John the Baptist.

If the delay is prompted by the Holy Spirit, then waiting for the right timing and opportunity is the wisest thing for a man to do. He can use the time serving his family as an incubation period for spiritual maturity. Besides, being a missionary at home provides "on the job" training for being a missionary to the rest of the world later. More than anywhere else, a man will be forced to develop a consistency between what he says and what he does—after all, his kids will call him on it in a heartbeat.

Set appropriate boundaries. Once a man decides to get involved in a ministry, he needs to work with his wife to set strict limits and expectations beforehand. Full-time pastors, missionaries, and men in counseling and support roles in particular must set safeguards to prevent encroachment on their family.

There are regions of grasslands and farmlands surrounding the Sahara Desert in Africa that have had vegetation growing on them for thousands of years. However, because of desertification—the expansion of the Sahara—the desert sands are constantly pushing southward and encroaching on these livable, arable lands. In the same way, without any barriers in place, church ministries can have a desertification effect of their own on a man's family life, encroaching little by little on the time and energy that should be oriented toward home.

To prevent this from happening, a man needs to set reasonable boundaries and have the courage to stick to them. The impact on a man's wife and children will be profound when he holds himself to his word. What's more, when an extraordinary crisis does arise and demand his immediate attention, his family will rally around him rather than resent yet another intrusion.

Check your motivation. Once a man begins to mature

in his faith, getting involved in the work of the church is a natural step in obedience. But we shouldn't kid ourselves; there are other factors. A man can flat out enjoy what he is doing. The enjoyment a man receives from this work is not a negative—it is, in fact, a confirmation of how serving God fulfills our deepest needs. But it does point to the fact that our motivations can become muddied.

Guilt can also be a motivating factor for a man's involvement. After all, if a man regularly attends a church, chances are high that he will be asked to get involved in a ministry. I vividly remember a lady in a church we attended many years ago who was famous for swooping through the church hallways like a hawk looking for an unwitting victim to fill a particular need. "A job needs to be done," she said, "so I need to find someone to do it." She was well-intentioned, but she had a way of talking people into saying "Yes" before they knew what hit them. "Prayerful consideration" was a luxury to her, but it is a necessity for a man of wisdom.

Aim to involve the entire family. Finally, a man should explore how he can pull off a coup—involving his entire family in a church ministry. While these opportunities can be rare, doing so is the best of all possible situations—reaching out to the world while at the same time bringing the family together in the process.

Once a man has paused his career and handcuffed his church ministry, he has opened up his heart and calendar to becoming an Expeditionary Man. However, there is another area of biblical manhood that men must consider—and one that will catch most everyone completely off guard.

CHAPTER 11

CAMP 3: INJECTING "DAD" IN EDUCATION

*That of all the men we meet with,
nine parts out of ten are what they are,
good or bad, useful or not,
according to their education.*
— John Locke

It's Friday morning, 9:05 a.m. I am sitting on a couch in our "homeschool room," an oblong space directly above our garage that we use for classes. My three boys are gathered around me as we discuss the history topic of the day. Jordan joins me on the couch, while Justy seats himself directly across on the floor. Jared sits beside him in a swivel office chair, desperately fighting the urge to spin around in circles during the discussion.

I start out keeping the talk focused on my list of questions, but eventually the three of them get off topic and debate medieval war tactics or some other boy-friendly subject. As they do so, I let my mind wander for a second and reflect on how surreal this scene is for me. Me teaching? I certainly did not see this one coming. A Bible study teacher or men's group leader? *Sure, I can do that.* A substitute junior high Sunday school teacher? *Oh, I suppose in a stretch.* But part-time school instructor of my three boys? *No way, that's not something I would ever do!*

One of the most contentious debates within Christian circles these days is the issue of schooling—public, private, or homeschool. Public school advocates believe that Christian kids are called to be in the world witnessing to their nonbelieving friends. Homeschoolers argue that the personalized instruction of a parent provides the ideal learning environment in which to thrive. Backers of Christian schools claim that they have the best of both worlds—safe Christian surroundings conducive to learning. I am not so much interested in that debate* as I am the issue of a man's hands-on role in *whichever* schooling option his family feels called to.

A Leadership Umbrella

Of all the topics in this book, participating in the education of their children is surely the one that seems less relevant, interesting, or compelling for most Christian men. It certainly was for me. I even toyed with whether this subject deserved to be given the same weight alongside the other life changes that a man needs to make in his quest for biblical manhood. Yet, as I reflect on the experiences of my own life, the tie-in among the four commitments—career, ministry, education, and discipleship—is inescapable. My role as part-time teacher is proving so integral to what we are striving for as a family, I could not downplay or avoid it.

---

* The schooling debate can be as rancorous and divisive as any within the church. However, as with many other modern-day issues that are not explicitly discussed in Scripture, each couple needs to seek God's counsel and make their decisions based on the direction and leading of the Holy Spirit.

This story unfolded soon after I began my authoring career at home. I had already made several major life decisions concerning my work and church involvement to ensure that I had the bandwidth necessary to devote myself to my family. Kim had been homeschooling the boys for years, but I never gave a second thought to being personally involved in what they were doing. That was her world. Education was a pivotal activity in the life of my boys, of course, but not something that seemed related to what I was trying to accomplish at home. My strategy at the time was classic "divide and conquer"—I would write books and disciple my boys, while Kim would teach them. But over the course of the next several months, I began to see the potency of a much different "leadership umbrella" strategy.

I think it is safe to say that every Christian man understands the importance of raising his children to have a relationship with Christ. He may not give enough priority to it or be particularly effective leading them, but he at least acknowledges the need. But, like me a number of years ago, few of these same men give any consideration to being actually involved in the education of their children. *That's someone else's job* is the unspoken assumption. For men who send their children to public or private schools, the schoolteachers have that responsibility. Homeschool dads are no different: the mother is in charge of instruction. I have been around dozens of homeschoolers over the years, and I know of only one father who does more than occasional math tutoring.

As men, I am convinced that we so easily delegate the responsibility of teaching to someone else because we consider education to be just about the three Rs—reading, 'riting, and 'rithmetic. That's why Christian parents nearly always base their schooling decisions on the quality of academics or the social environment their kids inhabit as they learn.

However, once I began teaching my boys, I realized how shortsighted I had always been. They were learning much more than simply how to do a geometry proof or how to write a thesis statement. Their education was establishing identity and purpose, building character, and shaping the way in which they viewed the world. I now understood what nineteenth-century Bishop J. C. Ryle was talking about when he said that a child's education, whether formal or informal, was a major determinant to the adult he or she would become: "But after nature and grace, undoubtedly, there is nothing more powerful than education. We are made what we are by training. Our character takes the form of that mould into which our first years are cast."

We have bought into the modern secular idea that education is man's great quest for discovering knowledge and truth. But as believers, we need to remind ourselves that the act of learning and discovery is not a human accomplishment. It's a God-breathed activity designed to prepare our minds and hearts to know him and his universe. That's why education, when viewed from a biblical perspective, will always integrate faith and learning. A Christian worldview becomes the bedrock for all instruction, enabling kids to grasp the reality that Jesus Christ lies behind everything they learn—from science, to math, to literature, to politics. In my case, I began to see that, although I was prepping my boys academically, I was doing so much more: education was emerging as a key component to preparing them for who they become in Christ.

As time went on, I was finding it more and more difficult to separate the biblical role of a father—as outlined in Deuteronomy, Proverbs, and the Pauline letters—from schooling. Suddenly, a man's involvement in teaching no longer seemed like a "Mr. Mom" activity, but a natural extension of a man's hands-on leadership role in the household.

I wish I could say that it was keen foresight and inspiration that led me to my participation in schooling my boys. But to be honest, the motivation was something far more practical and mundane. Since I was now in start-up mode in my new career and not getting a regular paycheck, Kim agreed to go back to work as a nurse for three nights a week. But in doing so, she needed me to cover her teaching responsibilities on the mornings after she worked. I reluctantly agreed to step in as the substitute teacher, helping out as needed and adjusting my work schedule around it. *This is not my sort of thing*, I thought, *but what other choice do I have?*

As the months passed, however, my reluctance turned into intrigue, and intrigue slowly turned into enthusiasm. This role, I realized, could be so much more than just a stop-gap measure; it was a chance for me to impact my boys' lives in a new arena. I stepped up my involvement by teaching one class, and then I added another the following semester. By the start of the next school year, my wife and I had completely transformed our schooling model—we were now doing a full-on, tag-team approach. I took over the morning classes and she took the other half in the afternoon. This new arrangement has enabled us both to participate on a daily basis, cover for each other when work conflicts, and teach to our strengths. My increased involvement greatly complicates my schedule, but I cannot conceive of doing anything else.

A man may need to do some creative scheduling to make it work, but the advantages of a father being involved with schooling are plenty. First, he is able to personally shepherd and steer the way in which faith is incorporated into all the subjects he teaches. A man should not be a "control freak," but as a father, he needs that control (in partnership with his wife) to bring his kids to spiritual maturity.

Second, as their teacher, a man gets an opportunity to interact with his children on a different level than as father. As he does so, he is able to experience another side of them that would otherwise be closed to him without that daily interaction.

Third, a man should teach all his children as one class whenever it makes sense to do so. Because you end up being together so much, a unity and a bond develops among siblings and the family as a whole that would never exist if everyone went their separate directions all week.*

Fourth, a man can have dedicated hours of structured time with his kids each weekday. While busyness, fatigue, and schedule conflicts can often push off impromptu family time, he has an obligation as their teacher to block

---

* Consider, for example, what happened to us last spring. My wife had an unexpected trip to Indiana to visit her mom in the hospital, leaving me all alone to school the boys for the week. However, on Friday, I had a meeting scheduled during the morning that I could not easily get out of. I could have had them work on their morning assignments on their own, but we came up with a more creative solution—a late night homeschool session. We read and discussed Shakespeare at 1:00 a.m. and then I heard the three do a formal ninety-minute debate on gun control at 2:00 a.m. As wacky as that sounds (and Kim thought we were nuts), the experience created a special intimacy among the four of us. The power of these "unforgettable moments" cannot be underestimated for a family climbing on an expedition together.

off those dedicated hours—either morning, afternoon, or night—for school classes.

Finally, the whole experience is personally rewarding. The challenge of instructing, guiding, and stretching his children becomes a genuine adventure for a man. In fact, in my case, I am not sure if there has been a more significant decision that I have made concerning my role as a father.

OBSTACLES

In spite of all of the advantages I have discovered from my experience, I can appreciate why so many men are reticent, reluctant, or downright resistant to teaching their children themselves. The two most common objections I hear from other men that I talk to are: "I don't have time," or "I can't do that."

I don't have time. The issue that immediately arises in a man's mind over increased involvement in his children's education is the lack of time to make it work. A man who lives at the office for much of the week struggles with just getting a dose of quality time with his family as it is. Therefore, the idea of committing himself in a substantive way to teaching sounds either improbable or unrealistic.

However, before a man dismisses the possibility outright, he should first back up and consider what opportunities might still be available for him. For public and private schoolers, a man should think outside the box as he attempts to find ways to immerse faith and a Christian worldview into what his children are learning at school. For homeschoolers, a man should consider a trial run by teaching a class in the evenings or on a Saturday. (In homeschool households, telecommuters, self-employed men, and guys working flex-time are particularly well positioned to creatively pack an hour of teaching into the flow of their day.)

I can't do that. The second objection that many have is the belief that they are not cut out for teaching their kids. Maybe they don't consider themselves patient or smart enough. Perhaps they don't think their kids will respond to them. Whatever the reason, lack of confidence alone should never hinder a man. "For when I am weak, then I am strong," Paul reminds us in 2 Corinthians 12:10. After all, in other parts of a man's life, he usually loves a challenge. Most men, for example, relish the opportunity of accepting a promotion at work that they don't feel fully prepared or qualified for. Or, for men involved in competitive amateur sports, they usually succeed only because they overachieve beyond their natural giftings.

In an era of educational choice, Christians are going to have honest disagreements on the best way to educate a child. But no matter if a couple chooses public school, private school, or homeschool, a man needs to weigh the costs of his time and energy with the possible return on that investment. The eighteenth-century Anglican pastor Richard Cecil reminds us what is at stake: "He has seen but little of life who does not discern everywhere the effect of education on men's opinions and habits of thinking. The children bring out of the nursery that which displays itself throughout their lives."

In the end, the educational component of biblical fatherhood is too important for a man not to be involved someway, somehow in the process (even if it is only in a guiding, advisory role). By starting out with modest goals and sticking to them for a semester or two, a man can take a watch-and-see approach to where God takes the experiment.

Think for a moment of the issues you see appearing regularly in the sports headlines. When a coveted NFL coach is hired, there is one issue that is always more important to the candidate than salary, contract length, or other factors—control. An elite NFL coach wants to be in an organization in which he has full authority, not just of what happens on the field, but also personnel and salary cap decisions for his team. They want this control, not as a power trip, but because they realize that their ability to achieve the goal of winning the Super Bowl depends on bringing a consistent, integrated approach across all aspects of the football operations.

In the same way, when a man injects himself into the education of his children, his ability to achieve his goal for his family—to climb their own Everest, so to speak—receives a turbo boost. His leadership umbrella is now able to extend over all key areas of family life rather than just parts of it. He can ensure that he (and his wife) are providing a consistent message and delivering an integrated approach to training and instruction in the Lord.

"Economies of scale" is a business term that refers to a production process in which an increase in the size of the company causes a decrease in the average cost of each unit produced. In laymen's terms, the more a company produces, the greater the return on investment. I am convinced that there is an equivalent "economy of scale" that a man can achieve when key parts of the day are shaped around his family.

The impact a man can have in thirty minutes of quality time a day with his family, quite frankly, will be modest. But when a man is able to consistently intermix structured, semistructured, and informal recreational time as a family, the overall impact on the lives of his children will be exponential. And, in doing so, a man has just created a lifestyle in which he can perform the most critical task of all en route to the summit—producing tomorrow's disciples.

CHAPTER 12

Camp 4: Producing Tomorrow's Disciples

*It's not the job of the church to be the main
force behind students' spiritual formation.
It is, and always has been, the role of parents.*
—Mike DeVries, YouthBuilders

Grit and determination, Everesters will tell you, are essential to enduring Camp 4 while the team awaits a break in the weather. At 25,500 feet, Camp 4 is the final inhabitable stop on the slopes of Everest and serves as the gateway to the summit. The camp, perched on the edge of the Death Zone, is a far more hostile living environment than the three camps below it. The arctic weather makes movement difficult, and hurricane-like winds chronically throw anything not tied down over the mountain's edge. The high altitude at Camp 4 also makes life unpredictable, threatening mental and physical problems for even the most experienced and physically fit climbers.

When it comes to discipling his children, a man needs the same grit and determination as these climbers. It's a tough commitment. Like trying to endure at Camp 4 on Everest, the stakes are never higher and choices that his children make are beyond his control. There are no formulas, no "Seven Habits to Discipleship Success," that guarantee the outcome. A man can cling to Proverbs 22:6 and live it out to the best of his ability, but even that passage doesn't promise a smooth ride along the way.

It is not surprising, then, that many Christian men feel inadequate about their ability to disciple their kids. Perhaps they don't feel knowledgeable enough of the Scriptures to teach. Maybe they don't know how to find the time in their schedule. Or maybe they feel as if they are a bad example for their kids. Whatever the reason, men often delegate this responsibility to the church — in particular, the youth pastor. It seems like a logical move. After all, youth ministries seem to have much more to offer than a father does — weekly meetings, Bible studies, youth rallies, summer camps, missions trips, and even a full-time staff.

Youth ministries can be great resources for parents, but a man should never relinquish to his church the control of and responsibility for the spiritual nurturing of his children. Youth programs are supplements, complementing what a father is already doing at home. If his children are getting the bulk of their spiritual meat and potatoes from the church, a man is not living up to his calling of biblical fatherhood.

A FATHER'S COMMISSION

An annual missions emphasis weekend is a regular staple at the churches I have attended over the course of my life. Banners on the wall exhort people to "Go beyond your borders" and "Pray global, act local." Wall maps with missionary photos sprinkled across the continents show others who are living out their calling now. When the pastor or visiting missionary speaks, it is almost certain that he will use Matthew 28:19–20 as the scriptural text: "Therefore go and make disciples of all nations, baptizing them in the name of the Father and of the Son and of the Holy Spirit, and teaching them to obey everything I have commanded you." Like clockwork, the speaker ends by calling on the congregation to live out this Great Commission in their lives—either overseas or in their local communities.

Christians are certainly called to go into the world for Christ as these mission weekends proclaim. But as I began to look at my family as my primary mission field, Christ's words took on a whole new light. I saw that the Great Commission also provides a solid roadmap for a man to produce tomorrow's disciples right inside his home. In other words, the same principles to which Christ calls us at a macro level are equally valid at the micro level.* Let me unpack the four action items from that passage.

Take initiative. Christ calls his disciples to "go," to proactively reach people who need to be ministered to. Obviously, an American missionary cannot expect to stay stateside and impact people in Africa. Instead, he needs to go directly to them, live in their communities, suffer when they suffer, and rejoice when they rejoice.

In the same way, a man is naïve if he expects his personal example of faith and devotion to rub off on his kids. Trickle-down discipleship does not work. Kids will cover themselves with a faith coating that lasts while they are home, but falls off as soon as they leave for college.

---

* Ironically, as a man fulfills the Great Commission inside his home, he is also indirectly living it out on the world stage as well. For when a man's children become disciples, they will, in turn, fulfill the Great Commission based on the Lord's calling in their lives.

Consequently, when a man disciples his children, he needs to follow Christ's words and take initiative, engaging and meeting his family where they are.

Bring to maturity. Christ instructs his followers in the Great Commission to "make disciples," not "make converts." The wording is significant. Christ's command indicates that a child's personal decision for Christ is just the starting line, not the end game. A man is, therefore, called to bring up his kids to a maturing, growing faith, not simply to evangelize them.

Make their faith their own. Christ instructs his listeners to "baptize" these new converts. The specific act of baptism is obviously an important milestone in the faith of a new believer, but I think there is another point a man can glean from this command. Baptism is, after all, a public declaration of a private faith. It's like getting a Christian ID badge, so to speak. Seen in that light, a man who disciples his children will encourage them to identify themselves with Christ as they make their faith their own.

Train them in Christ. Finally, a man living out the Great Commission in his home will train his children in obedience to the words of Christ himself. But in doing so, he needs to know exactly where his kids are spiritually and tailor his instruction based on their maturity level.

During the early years of a child's life, the primary purpose of a parent's influence is simply to establish a foundation of love, affection, trust, and emotional stability. I call this the *nurturing stage*, and usually the mother will take the lead in this early time of a child's life. Next, during the *teaching stage*, as the child gets older and enters elementary and middle school years, a man's responsibility to train and instruct takes root as he grounds his children in biblical truth and establishes a biblical worldview. The goal for a man at this point is to put the child in a position to make a decision to believe in Jesus Christ.

Finally, as the child starts the high school years, a man enters the critical *enabling stage*. The purpose of a father's training in this stage is to transform child-believers into battle-ready disciples. Their faith needs to evolve from a replica of their parents' faith into a sustainable version all its own.

During this final stage, a man needs to walk a fine line between being too restrictive and too lenient. In order to "enable" his kids, he needs to progressively allow them certain degrees of freedom in decision making, all the while maintaining a safety net when things go awry. If a father is in touch with his kids, he will know the type of decisions they are ready for and the ones they are not.

A father and mother obviously have integral roles to play in each of these stages. But the God-given strengths and biblical responsibilities of the mother usually have her taking the lead during the nurturing stage, while father's guiding role needs to peak during the teaching and enabling stages.

SAVVY LEADERSHIP

During the earthly ministry of Jesus, the disciples often seemed to exhibit the clumsiness of Inspector Clouseau. They frequently put their foot in their mouths, doing or saying the wrong things at the wrong time. Yet, by the time these apostles were filled with the Holy Spirit and were ready to go out into world and fulfill the Great Commission, they were totally different people. Their transformed faith and allegiance to Christ gave them a wisdom that helped them shed their bumbling nature to successfully preach the gospel throughout the Roman world.

As they carried out their roles as evangelists and church planters, they did so with remarkable skill and proficiency: tailoring the gospel message to their particular audience, establishing churches, exercising leadership that would survive beyond them, and so on. This is exactly the sort of savvyness a man needs to bring to his discipleship efforts at home as he plays three distinct leadership roles — a culture maker, a guide, and a unifier.

Culture Maker

If I were to throw out the question "How are you discipling your kids?" to a men's group, I suspect the typical answers would be something like "We hold a weekly Bible study," "I lead a family prayer time," or "I take my kids out weekly to talk." Men are problem solvers, after all. So we tend to look at discipling as a set of tasks that we can work into our calendar. Family devotions, one-on-one talks, and prayer times are great activities, but they will usually prove ineffective if they stand on their own. The pitfall of an activity-based approach to family discipleship is that a man ends up segregating "discipleship" from "normal life." To kids, discipleship becomes "that thing that Dad leads at 8:00 p.m. on Wednesdays," just before they get to watch *Lost*.

In contrast, the practical teaching of Deuteronomy 6:6–9 tells a far different story. A man is to teach God's Word to his children by talking about it everywhere (at home and on the road) and anytime (at night and in the morning). Seen in this light, *discipleship is not divorced from normal life; it is the very definition of normal life.*

The implicit message of Scripture is that a man is charged with establishing a "culture of discipleship" inside his home, in which faith is integral to everything going on. When such an environment exists, everything a family does is a discipling opportunity—meal conversations, songs played, movies watched, and attitudes expressed around the home. A culture of discipleship demonstrates the reality of God's hand in all situations and reinforces the need for a person's faith to impact their behavior and attitudes in the most common of situations. When this culture permeates a family, Bible studies, prayer time, and impromptu faith discussions no longer seem unnatural and out of context of everyday life.

Here is exactly where the investment of hands-on leadership pays off. The only kind of father who will be successful in "making culture" in his household is one who is fully engaged and has street cred. He must be *hands-on* to be in a position to influence the family culture, and he must be seen by his wife and kids as a *leader* to have the influence necessary to actually pull it off.

Guide

Once a man establishes a culture of discipleship, he needs to be savvy in the way in which he communicates biblical teaching to his kids. The apostle Paul's relationship with the church in Thessalonica provides a great model for a man to emulate. The family connection is not lost on Paul either, as he compares the way in which he acted toward the Thessalonians with parents acting toward their children. Check out what Paul says in 1 Thessalonians 2:6–12 (italics mine):

> ... as apostles of Christ we could have asserted our prerogatives. Instead, we were like young children among you.

Just as a nursing mother cares for her children, so we cared for you. *Because we loved you so much, we were delighted to share with you not only the gospel of God but our lives as well.* Surely you remember, brothers and sisters, our toil and hardship; we worked night and day in order not to be a burden to anyone while we preached the gospel of God to you.

You are witnesses, and so is God, of *how holy, righteous and blameless we were among you who believed.* For you know that we dealt with each of you as *a father deals with his own children, encouraging, comforting and urging you to live lives worthy of God,* who calls you into his kingdom and glory.

In verse 8, Paul begins by talking about how he came to the Thessalonian church to share not only the gospel, but also his life. Paul did not lead as a hands-off bishop; rather, he invested his life into the church because of his love for them. In economics, "to invest" means to put money at risk for the purpose of making a profit. When a man lives up to Paul's example and invests himself in his family, he shares and risks himself—his time, career, and opportunities—for the purpose of making disciples.

Next, Paul says in verse 10 that he was "holy, righteous and blameless" when he was among them. Similarly, a man must be aware that, like it or not, he is a role model for his children, leading by example more than by words (1 Cor. 11:1). What he says during a family devotion hour is far less significant to a child's faith than how he responds during a crisis.

When a man loses his temper, how does he respond? When he wrongs his kids, how quickly does he apologize to them? When he loses his job, does he panic or calmly respond in faith? When he has a moral dilemma, does he seek expediency or does he use it as a showcase example for his children? I think back to my childhood and remember being aware of the amount of time I saw Dad studying the Bible or spending time in prayer. Even today, my sister vividly remembers the impression this left on her: "The image of Dad in his prayer chair will forever be etched in my mind."

Continuing on in 1 Thessalonians 2:11 – 12, Paul encourages and exhorts the believers in the Thessalonian church to live lives worthy of God. When a man motivates his children in their Christian walk, he must be equally savvy as Paul was in his approach. He needs to avoid preaching, hounding, and chastising to get results (Eph. 6:4). Instead, he should continually encourage, comfort, and cheer his kids on to produce lasting change. Rather than have a face-to-face confrontation with his children over their failures, he continually "encourages," or comes alongside his children. As a man does so, he invites them to see the world from his perspective and makes himself available to take the lead in times of need.

Unifier

In even the best of families, attitudes have a way of hardening and biting sarcasm can creep up in everyday conversations. When left unchecked, these feelings will produce discord, kill personal growth, and eventually turn into bitterness and isolation. That's why a man is called to take the role of unifier as a key part of his discipleship efforts. When I speak of a unifier, I am not talking about just a "peacemaker," someone trying to keep the peace. Instead, a man needs to build and preserve a true unity and bond, not simply work for the absence of conflict.

When a family grows into a "little church," as the Puritans called it, a Christ-centered unity is a natural by-product (John 17:21–23). Consider how Paul encourages the church in Ephesus toward this same union: "Make every effort to keep the unity of the Spirit through the bond of peace" (Eph. 4:3). The spiritual maturation that makes this possible is discussed a few verses later in verse 14. Children are "tossed back and forth by the waves, and blown here and there by every wind of teaching and by the cunning and craftiness of people in their deceitful scheming." However, as a man disciples them, they will begin to "reach unity in the faith and in the knowledge of the Son of God and become mature, attaining to the whole measure of fullness of Christ." Continuing on, in verse 16, Paul brings the discussion full circle by talking about the unity that results: each part of the body is "joined and held together by every supporting ligament, grows and builds itself up in love."

In my quest for biblical manhood, I occasionally reflect on the lower mountain that I have climbed with my family and see the life changes I have made in each of the "camps"—career, ministry, education, and discipleship. As I do so, however, I often catch myself looking backward to see exactly what kind of trail marks I am leaving in my path. Am I forging a path that will last forever, or will it quickly be covered over by drifting snow?

A View from
the Summit

What you do now echoes in eternity.

—Maximus, *Gladiator*

A man is hardwired for adventure. Perhaps it is not surprising, then, that many men spend their entire lives sprinting forward in pursuit of what makes their pulse race and blood flow. Professional success, changed lives in ministry, creative works of art, sporting competitions—you name it. However, once in a while, a man cannot help but stop, turn his head around, and look at the trail behind him. He wants to know that the struggles and sacrifices he has made in pursuit of these exploits do matter. Therefore, as powerful as adventure is to a man, it cannot survive on its own. No, there is a flipside to adventure that is equally important—significance. A man craves adventure, but he needs one that really means something in the long run.

You see this truth played out in the life of climber Reinhold Messner, which is ironic because his life motto—*I am what I do*—seems to deny the need for any long-term significance. Messner is considered by many to be the greatest mountain climber of all time. He was the first to solo-climb Everest without supplemental oxygen in 1980, a feat that many considered impossible. He was also the first person to climb all the world's "eight-thousanders," the fourteen peaks above 8,000 meters (or 26,000 feet). But even Messner discovered that these sorts of solo adventures, by themselves, do not satisfy. "When I finished the 8,000-meter peaks, I understood, now I could only repeat myself," said Messner. "What I did is boring now. But I like to go somewhere where everything is new, and to begin again an activity." As such, he gave up climbing mountains and now looks for new adventures by taking expeditions to the most remote regions of the earth.

Messner reminds me of a modern-day Sisyphus, the mythical king who is destined to forever roll a huge rock up a hill only to have it fall down again. Messner is continually "pushing" an adventure up a slope. But as he gets to the top, it falls back down before he experiences any lasting meaning or fulfillment from what he just performed. His adventures, as incredible as they may be, are disposable to him. They are nothing more than a "been there, done that." As a result, in order to live, he has to move on to the next adventure. Reflecting on this outlook, his brother Hansjorg wonders whether Reinhold may also believe an opposite motto: *If I cease to do, I will not be.*

Reinhold Messner is not alone. As I have openly shared in this book, I was an adventure junkie for many years of my life. I was relentless in pursuing the Next Great Opportunity through my job and always seemed to have a stockpile full of ventures. The dotcom boom only added fuel to my fire when entrepreneurial ideas, start-up opportunities, and blockbuster IPOs were swarming around

Silicon Valley. Everyone with ambition was looking for that "killer idea" to jump on board with and go public.

However, even though I was in the midst of this exhilarating storm and at the peak of my professional success, I felt empty. I couldn't help but stop and turn my head to view the trail dust behind me. But when I looked around, I was chilled by what I saw ... there was nothing, no lasting legacy at all. *I am consumed with identifying the next hot technology and revolutionizing the Web,* I admitted to myself. *But am I doing anything at all that has eternal significance?*

God has an impeccable sense of timing. At the same time I was wrestling with these questions, Paramount finally released the Oscar-winning film *Braveheart* on DVD. Because it is one of my all-time favorite movies, I purchased the DVD on the day it came out. As I sat down to watch it, I found myself initially captivated and eventually haunted by a single line spoken by Mel Gibson. You'll recall the scene in which William Wallace is in prison on the night before he is to be executed. Princess Isabelle comes in to talk with him and to try to give him poison so he won't have to face the pain of torture the next day. When she talks of her fear over his death, he replies, "Every man dies; not every man really lives."

Oh, I had heard that line before, but I felt as if Gibson was delivering that line to me personally as I watched it this time around. *What does "really lives" mean?* I wondered. *Am I living a life that matters? Or is my time that I am spending on earth a "ho hum" in light of eternity?*

Significance is such a tricky thing to have a proper perspective on in the present tense. The things that matter to me so much today are, by and large, forgotten about days, months, and almost certainly years from now. I look back and think about things that occupied my time a decade ago. My software baby—a software product I dedicated all of my creative energies to—is long gone. No one uses it any more. Even the company I committed my heart to is no longer around.

Suppose, in cleaning my attic, I stumble across a magic "do over" pencil. Using this supernatural device, I am able to return to earlier times in my life to erase activities that proved insignificant and pencil in activities that I should have done instead. Silly idea, I admit, but you get the point: a look to the past is the best gauge to determining what is really important now. We are rarely objective in the moment.

Kim and I traveled to England several years ago for our anniversary and had a chance to spend two nights at Eastwell Manor, a castle hotel that has a history spanning over nine hundred years. Each of the rooms in the hotel is named after a person associated with the manor. We stayed in the Robert Curtoys room. Robert was the eldest son of William the Conqueror, an army general, and one of the first owners of Eastwell Manner in 1099. As I read through a small booklet in the room describing his colorful life and dangerous exploits against King Henry I, I was struck by the importance of his adventures as the centuries pass. Not only was his short life a brief flicker in the span of human history, but his legacy today seems little more than a placard on a second story corner room of an aging stone castle.

I am a film buff and have a love for the classic films from the Golden Age of Hollywood. Movie stars during this era were larger than life, and in the center of the glamour stage was Humphrey Bogart. Bogie was a superstar; he was not only adored by ladies, but he was a "man's man" as well. His career had everything an actor could ever want: over twenty major films, an Academy award, and a starring role in some of the greatest films ever. One of my all-time favorite roles in film is Bogart's portrayal of Rick Blaine, the cynical bar owner in *Casablanca*. Yet, as much of a fan as I am, I have to admit that, in today's era of postmodern realism, his acting style looks archaic and his tough-guy characterizations seem cliché. Hollywood has long since passed him by.

No professional athlete has ever walked away from his sport better than John Elway did. Elway was a perennial all-pro quarterback and considered by many to be the greatest clutch player in the history of the game. He retired at the peak of his success—winning back-to-back Super Bowls and receiving the Super Bowl MVP award. My favorite memory of Elway was seeing him play at Mile High Stadium in a divisional playoff game back in 1992. It was perhaps the most thrilling moment I've ever experienced in sports when, with 1:46 left on the clock, Elway single-handedly took his team down the field seventy-six yards to defeat the Houston Oilers 26–24. I remember the chants of "Elway! Elway!" filling the stadium as he walked off in celebration. But now, years removed from the Elway era, those chants have long since died. His gridiron legacy, as great as it was, has become an NFL films highlight reel and a bust in Canton.

Closer to home is a man I'll call Ted Jones, an elder at a church we once attended. He possessed a strong sense of authority and genuine humility—a rare combination that made him the prototype of the servant leader. Yet, the leadership hat he loved to wear at church rarely made it through the front door of his home. His business stole his time and his church stole his heart, leaving little time leftover for his family. Ted will leave a legacy of impacting people's lives at his church, but the impact on his only child remains a question mark to this day. His thirty-year-old son is now walking far from the Lord and has no interest in coming back.

When I look at the lasting influence of these men, I am struck by the realization that a man's earthly legacy becomes more and more two-dimensional as the years pass. Robert Curtoys is but a Wikipedia entry, Bogart is reduced to images on a strip of cellulose, and John Elway is a name on the Mile High Ring of Fame. I am reminded of a scene in the movie *Breach* in which an FBI agent sums up his legacy at the agency when he retires, "I could stay there another hundred years and still just be an afterthought ... But I'll get my portrait on that twenty-five year wall, right? Now that's something." *Is it really, Mr. Hanssen?* I asked myself when watching the film. *Who really cares about a retiree's picture on a wall?* Time has a nasty way of flattening a man so that he will fit conveniently into a newspaper obit, an investment portfolio, or a wall portrait.

There is another type of legacy, however...

Every man who decides to live as an Expeditionary Man will have a new role to play, a new adventure to pursue, and a new summit to climb. But as he does this, something else happens: his life takes on a new significance. His legacy is changed from something flat into something three-dimensional; it becomes more than a static memory of the past, but a dynamic, real-time, ongoing heritage that survives forever. Above all, it becomes exactly what Maximus is driving at in *Gladiator* when he utters that great line, "What you do now echoes in eternity."

In this cookie-cutter world, every man is far more replaceable than what he would like to think he is. Robert Curtoys and Humphrey Bogart were soon outdone by greater army generals and better actors. Even the legend of John Elway is slowly being surpassed by the likes of Tom Brady, Peyton Manning, and Brett Favre. When I resigned from a company several years ago, I secretly hoped that I would get an email from a coworker a month or two later that said something like, *Boy, we need you back . . . You were so much better than the new guy . . . It's just not the same anymore.* No, I never got that email. I too was far more replaceable than I imagined.

Surprisingly, this truth holds for a man in service to Jesus Christ. God may use me as an author to reach thousands of people through my books, as a teacher at my church to disciple dozens of others, and perhaps someday even as a missionary to minister to many people in Haiti. But God has plenty of other authors, teachers, and missionaries at his disposal. If he does not use me, he can certainly use someone else to get the job done.

But I have one calling in which I am considered irreplaceable in the eyes of the Lord—as a father. God does not mix and match here; he never willingly sends in a replacement. As the father of my three sons, I am the *only* one in this universe positioned to live out the principles of Deuteronomy 6:5–7 and Proverbs 22:6 with them. I am the *only* one to whom God has entrusted this adventurous responsibility of guiding Jordan, Jared, and Justus from childhood to adulthood. My wife is right alongside me as a partner, of course, but our father and mother roles are clearly distinct in Scripture. We complement rather than override each other. A mother or another relative can compensate and fill in if a father is not living out his calling, but it's never the same.

In the end, the lasting significance a man hungers for is gained by establishing an unquenchable faith in the soul of his kids. Then, once that legacy is firmly on track and managed, a man can begin to impact the rest of the world.

TESTING POINTS

Men like action films goes the cliché. While there is certainly truth to that, I think what men really love are those movies that strive for something beyond the ordinary, beyond the normal, beyond the safe. The main protagonist battles against a more powerful opponent and eventually faces a life-changing dilemma. At the climax of the film, he usually is forced to risk everything no matter the odds.

We cheer on Maximus in *Gladiator* when he decides to overthrow Emperor Commodus and William Wallace as he stands up to the English king in *Braveheart*—even if they are unsuccessful in their attempts. In *Field of Dreams*, we see a bit of ourselves in Ray Kinsella when he lives his dream and risks his farm and livelihood in the process. We are humbled by the selflessness of Frodo in *The Lord of the Rings* when he goes on his long journey to Mount Doom. We admire the longsuffering of *The Shawshank Redemption*'s Andy Dufresne and his outright refusal to lose hope in the most dreary of places. Finally, in our age of moral relativism, we are convicted by the integrity and character of Robert Roy MacGregor in the film *Rob Roy* when he risks his life purely for the sake of his honor.

None of these characters are perfect; they are all flawed people who make mistakes. But each of them has one common element that every man is instinctively attracted to—courage. "Courage is not simply one of the virtues," said C. S. Lewis, "but the form of every virtue at the testing point ... A chastity or honesty, or mercy, which yields to danger will be chaste or honest or merciful only on conditions. Pilate was merciful till it became risky." A man wants to be able to ante up and demonstrate raw courage at the testing points of his life. He wants that same greatness to be manifest in himself as he sees in Maximus, William Wallace, and Rob Roy.

When confronted with the issues I have been discussing in this book—pausing a career, limiting ministries, becoming a hands-on leader at home—every man will have a different testing point and require a different dose of courage if he decides to follow through. I think of several dedicated Christian men across the country facing a test right now.

Jerry is a highly successful director at his company, and for over a decade, he has bought into the idea of a balanced life. He has not been overly successful at doing so, but he is fearful of putting his career on hold, even though he knows what is at stake with his family. *Courage avoids wishful thinking.* Frank, by contrast, is far less passionate about his job than Jerry is. But up until now, he has accepted his daily two-hour commute and frequent travel without question. "That's why they call it work," he quips. However, with his kids entering high school, he is beginning to seriously consider other options. *Courage never settles for the status quo.*

Lee has always been the "go-to guy" at his church. When something needs to get done, everyone knows Lee is the one to call. That's why the idea of setting limits to his ministry involvement so he can become the "go-to guy" at home really bothers him. He feels much better suited for his church role and receives far more validation from these activities than he ever does from his demanding wife at home. *Courage is the willing pursuit of an adventure that goes unappreciated.*

Kevin is a regular in his men's accountability group. But he admits that the zeal and good intentions he conveys when he is with other men rarely seems to make its way home. Once inside his house, he describes himself as morphing into a caricature, an out-of-touch dad of a teenage son and daughter who live a lifestyle no different from their unbelieving neighbors. *Courage is putting belief into action.* Bill, however, wants something more out of life. He is not content with spending his days in an office job that does not produce anything of lasting value. Yet rather than minister to his houseful of children today, he confesses that his gut instinct is to retreat to his study and dream of becoming a full-time urban missionary tomorrow. *Courage is living out your primary calling.*

Javier is a sportsaholic. If he's not watching his favorite teams play, he is tuning to ESPN or listening to sports talk radio. If you spend five minutes with him, you'll discover all the trivia you will ever want to know about the history of the NBA. He feels burdened to be more involved in the lives of his three daughters, but he still would love to figure out a way to accomplish that goal without giving up any of his televised sports. *Courage is sacrificial.* Sam, in contrast, could care less about baseball or basketball. But he struggles with producing the drive and the initiative needed to build a team at home and lead them on a common adventure. Sam is frank about his decision if you talk to him. He admits that he much prefers the path of least resistance and just letting things stay as they are. *Courage is active, not passive.*

Finally, Ed feels handcuffed. He has two overachieving kids who are heavily involved in athletics, band, and the honors program at their school. Ed has observed for some time how their non-stop, after-school activities splinter the family and constantly send them off in separate directions. But Ed is wondering how he can now curb these extracurricular activities without cheating his children out of what they love and making them resentful of him. *Courage is making unpopular decisions.*

Each of these men certainly wants to be a good father and is committed to raising his children as believers. But the trick is turning this heartfelt desire into deliberate, decisive action. Will each of these men be willing to reach into their suitcase of courage to make a change when genuine sacrifice and risk are involved? I am reminded of something that nineteenth-century philosopher John Stuart Mill once wrote (italics mine):

> All Christians believe that the blessed are the poor and humble; that it is easier for a camel to pass through the eye of a needle than for a rich man to enter the kingdom of heaven ... They are not insincere when they say that they believe these things. They do believe them, as people believe what they have always heard lauded and never discussed. *But in the sense of that living belief that regulates conduct, they believe these doctrines just up to the point to which it is usual to act upon them.*

Of course, every Christian man believes he should sacrifice for his family and dedicate himself to training his children in their faith. We will heartily shout "amen" when we hear a conference speaker discussing the principles of biblical fatherhood. But we all struggle with believing these principles just up to the point to which we must act on them. Those six in ten kids who grow up in Christian homes and later turn their backs on Christ will back me up on that.

FROM A BEACH TO A SUMMIT

The adventurer in me would love nothing more than to conquer Mount Everest in my lifetime. My heart skips a beat when I read the words of British climbing legend George Mallory describing Everest to his wife in 1923: "Suffice it to say that [Everest] has the most steep ridges and appalling precipices that I have ever seen, and that all the talk of an easy snow slope is a myth ... My darling, this is a thrilling business altogether, I can't tell you how it possesses me, and what a prospect it is. And the beauty of it all!"

I would love to feel the sense of anticipation building as I go through several weeks of acclimatization, ascending and descending the lower parts of the mountain. To persevere with an expeditionary team as we climb and belay together, dependent on each other for survival. To feel that impulse of half-terror, half-excitement in my tent at Camp 4 on the night before a summit attempt. And then to rejoice in the raw exhilaration of walking those last steps onto the highest point on planet Earth. I imagine doing a 360-degree turn looking first into Nepal and then into Tibet, witnessing a sea of snow-covered mountains and brown plains that span hundreds of miles.

I am enough of a realist, however, to know that climbing Everest will stay a dream. The truth is that only a handful of people ever manage to get on a team to climb Everest, and fewer still ever get to conquer it.

But there is another view — one far more breathtaking than even the panorama of Everest. And this scene, on top of the *real* Rooftop of the World, will be seen by every believer someday in heaven. For some men, the view from that heavenly summit will seem strangely familiar, as if they could not have imagined it any other way. It will be the culmination of everything that they had been climbing toward during their earthly life. For other men, however, the mountain will seem alien, far different than the molehills of career and misplaced priorities they were hiking on by themselves back on earth.

The key question every man needs to ask himself when he considers that future mountain is who else will be standing next to him on the summit. Will he ascend to that summit as a solo climber? Or will he be an expeditionary guide, joined, sooner or later, by his wife, children, and grandchildren?

In this culture of self-determination, a man takes pride in the idea of being able to call the shots, to have the freedom to make the choices that impact his life. But the reality is that for the vast majority of a man's life, he makes few decisions of long-term importance. You can, in fact, usually count them on a hand or two. More often than not, he goes with the flow and does what's expected of him. But a few times in the life of a man, a crisis, need, or opportunity escalates to such an extent that he actually considers a major life change. If he has the courage to do so, his life is forever altered. But if he procrastinates, the issue is quickly swept under the rug and his auto-piloted life resumes.

I am reminded of a scene in *Changing Lanes* in which the main character, Gavin Banek, reflects on a moral dilemma he faces. Gavin is an attorney who has evidence in his possession that proves that he and his father-in-law boss did something unethical and illegal. His father-in-law and wife are strongly pressuring him to cover up the incident. He has two options. The safe route is to sell out, destroy the evidence, and go shopping for a yacht with his father-in-law. The risky option is to turn himself in and face disbarment. Gavin explains his dilemma:

> It's like you go to the beach. You go down to the water. It's a little cold. You're not sure if you want to go in. There's a pretty girl standing next to you. She doesn't want to go in either. She sees you, and you know that if you just asked her her name, you would leave with her. Forget your life, whoever you came with, and leave the beach with her. And after that day, you remember. Not every day, every week ... she comes back to you. It's the memory of another life you could have had. Today is that girl.

In the end, every man is facing a similar choice—whether to play it safe and do business as usual or to risk everything in Christ for his family. As Gavin puts it, "Today is that girl." Today, you have the opportunity to gather your family together and forget about your former life. Today, you have the opportunity to cast aside solo exploits, cultural norms, and the myth of a Balanced Life. Today, you have the opportunity to begin a whole new adventure ... the life of an Expeditionary Man.

ENDNOTES

CHAPTER 1:
HARDWIRED FOR ADVENTURE

Page 15: *Entertainment Software Association*, "2005 Sales, Demographics, and Usage Data: Essential Facts about the Computer and Video Game Industry." ("Heads of households" equals 60 percent male and 40 percent female.)

Page 16: Bill Simmons, "Feeling Like Clooney: Magictimes in Beantown." Posted October 2007 at http://sports.espn.go.com/espn/page2/story?page=simmons/071012&sportCat=nfl.

Page 17: David Chute and Mark Horowitz, "The 50 Best Guy Movies of All Time." Posted December 2003, at www.mensjournal.com/feature/0312/guymovies.html.

Page 20: David McCasland, *Oswald Chambers: Abandoned to God* (Grand Rapids: Discovery House, 1993), 225.

Page 26: Ibid., 156.

PART 1:
CLIMBING SOLO

Page 29: Permission granted for this song quote.

CHAPTER 2:
PUSHED AND PULLED

Page 34: Thomas F. Hornbein, *Everest: The West Ridge* (Seattle: Mountaineers Books, 1980), 28.

Page 37: Jon Krakauer, *Into Thin Air: A Personal Account of the Mount Everest Disaster* (New York: Villard, 1997), 68.

Page 38: Elizabeth A. Moize, "Daniel Boone: First Hero of the Frontier," *National Geographic* (Dec. 1985), 819. As quoted in

Weldon Hardenbrook, *Missing From Action* (Nashville: Nelson, 1987), 46.

Page 41: Robert Bly, *Iron John: A Book about Men* (New York: Vintage, 1992), 96–97. As quoted in Marc Porter Zasada, "Dad's Dilemma: Homeschooling Roles for the Full-Time Breadwinner." Posted 2006, www.homeschoolnewslink.com/homeschool/columnists/zasada/vol7iss1_UrbanMan.shtml.

Page 41: Weldon Hardenbrook, *Missing from Action* (Nashville: Nelson, 1987), 70.

Page 41: Lawrence Fuchs, *Family Matters* (New York: Random House, 1972), 109. As quoted in Hardenbrook, *Missing From Action*, 70.

Page 42: Marc Porter Zasada, "Dad's Dilemma."

Page 42: Becky Barrow, "19 Minutes—How Long Working Parents Give Their Children," *London Daily Mail*. Posted July 19, 2006, www.dailymail.co.uk/pages/live/articles/news/news.html?in_article_id=396609&in_page_id=1770.

Page 42: Kevin Smith, "Dad—More Than Just a Breadwinner," *Joy!* Posted February 2006, www.joymag.co.za/mag/2–2006/dads.php.

Page 48: Krakauer, *Into Thin Air*, as noted by Beck Weathers, *Left for Dead: My Journey Home from Everest* (New York: Random, 2001), ch. 3.

Page 51: Lou Whittaker, *Lou Whittaker: Memoirs of a Mountain Guide* (Seattle: Mountaineers Books, 1994), 160–61.

CHAPTER 3:
FROSTBITTEN FAMILIES

Page 53: Linkin Park, "Numb," *Meteora* (Warner Bros., 2003).

Page 59: Ed Vitagliano, "A Strange Faith—Are Church-Going Kids Christian?" *Agape Press*. Posted November 15, 2005, www.headlines.agapepress.org/archive/11/152005a.asp.

Page 59: Ibid.

Page 60: Lou Whittaker, *Lou Whittaker*, 160–61.

Page 65: Jon Krakauer, *Into Thin Air*, 210.

Page 65: Peter Potterfield, "Everest '97." *Mountain Zone*. Posted April 20, 1997, classic.mountainzone.com/everest/boukreev.stm.

CHAPTER 4:
FROM SOLO CLIMBER TO TEAM LEADER

Page 71: Jochen Hemmleb, Larry A. Johnson, and Eric R. Simonson, *Ghosts of Everest: The Search for Mallory and Irvine* (Seattle: Mountaineers Books, 1999), 25–26.

Page 72: Douglas Jones, "God the Riddler," *Credenda Agenda* 14, no. 1; www.credenda.org/issues/14–1poetics.php.

Page 74: William Blake, "Great Things Are Done."

Page 74: Jochen Hemmleb et al., *Ghosts of Everest*, 23.

Page 77: Jon Krakauer, *Into Thin Air*, 78.

Page 77: Jochen Hemmleb et al., *Ghosts of Everest*, 23.

Page 77: Joel Connelly, "In the Northwest: Pete Schoening to Be Forever Remembered for the Belay," *Seattle Post-Intelligencer*. Posted September 24, 2004, seattlepi.nwsource.com/connelly/192240_joel24.html.

Page 78: Charles Houston, *K2: The Savage Mountain* (Guilford, Conn.: Lyons, 2000).

Page 79: Ed Viesturs with Dave Roberts, *No Shortcuts to the Top: Climbing the World's 14 Highest Peaks* (New York: Broadway, 2006), 29.

Page 80: Mark Synnott, "How to Send Your Career," *Epic Magazine*. Posted on August 1, 2007, www.exploreepic.com/resources/200707/guidecareer.php.

Page 81: Peter Potterfield, "Dave Hahn: At the Top of His Game," *GreatOutdoors.com*. Posted 2007, www.greatoutdoors.com/published/climb/profiles/davehahn

Page 84: Lou Whittaker, *Lou Whittaker*, 177.

CHAPTER 5:
BEYOND THE SHERPA

Page 89: Ed Viesturs with Dave Roberts, *No Shortcuts to the Top*, 160.

Page 90: John MacArthur, "God's Pattern for Husbands Part 2: Ephesians 5:25, 29." Posted October 27, 2004, www.cbmw.org/Resources/Sermons/God-s-Pattern-for-Husbands-Part-2.

Page 91: Willard F. Harley Jr., *His Needs, Her Needs: Building an Affair-Proof Marriage* (Grand Rapids: Revell, 2001), 183.

Page 91: Dan Edelen, "The Real American Christian 'Either/Or.'" Posted August 16, 2006, www.ceruleansanctum.com/2006/08/the-real-american-christian-eitheror.html.

Page 91: "Stay at Home Dads," Posted November 13, 2006, thegospelshowonevoice.com/Pieces/?p=234.

CHAPTER 6:
TIGHTROPE DISCIPLESHIP

Page 103: Kari Grady Grossman, "Into the Icefall." Posted April 17, 2002, http://dsc.discovery.com/convergence/everest/dispatches/dispatch08.html.

Page 107: Dietrich Bonhoeffer, *The Cost of Discipleship* (New York: Collier, 1963), 62–63.

Page 110: Story based on "Faith Hall of Fame," www.eaec.org/faith hallfame/georgemuller.htm.

Page 111: Ruth Tucker, *From Jerusalem to Irian Jaya: A Biographical History of Christian Missions* (Grand Rapids: Zondervan, 2004), 173.

Page 115: Bonhoeffer, *The Cost of Discipleship*, 67.

Page 115: C. S. Lewis, *Mere Christianity* (San Francisco: HarperOne, 2001), 23.

Page 123: Edmund S. Morgan, *The Puritan Family* (New York: Harper Perennial, 1942), 139.

Page 123: Dr. C. Matthew McMahon, "The Christian Family," *A Puritan's Mind;* www.apuritansmind.com/TheChristianFamily/ChristianFamilyMainPage.htm.

Page 123: John Cotton, *The Way of Life* (1641); as quoted in Morgan, *The Puritan Family*, 7.

CHAPTER 7:
WINDOWS OF OPPORTUNITY

Page 127: G.K. Chesterton, *Heretics*, ch. 14. www.worldwideschool.org/library/books/lit/socialcommentary/Heretics/chap14.html.

Page 128: Silas Shotwell, *Homemade* (September, 1987); widely available on the Internet; see, e.g., http://net.bible.org/illustration.php?topic=1668.

Page 128: Ibid.

Page 135: C. S. Lewis, *The Screwtape Letters* (San Francisco: Harper-One, 2001), 60.

Page 135: J. C. Ryle, *Duties of Parents*, Part 3. Public domain, www.wholesomewords.org/family/ryleduties.pdf.

Page 136: Christian Smith, *Soul Searching: The Religious and Spiritual Lives of American Teenagers* (New York: Oxford University Press, 2005), 56–57.

Page 139: William Tecumseh Sherman, *Memoirs of General W. T. Sherman* (New York: Penguin, 2000), 758.

CHAPTER 8:
THRIVING IN THE DEATH ZONE

Page 143: "Everest: The Death Zone." NOVA. Original air date: February 24, 1998. Transcript. www.pbs.org/wgbh/nova/transcripts /2506everest.html.

Page 145: Ibid.

Page 147: Dietrich Bonhoeffer, *The Cost of Discipleship* (New York: Collier, 1963), 99.

CHAPTER 9:
CAMP #1: PAUSING YOUR CAREER

Page 171: Oswald Chambers, ed. Harry Verploegh, *Oswald Chambers: The Best from All His Books*, 2 vols. (Nashville: Nelson, 1987), 1:58.

CHAPTER 10:
CAMP 2: LIMITING YOUR MINISTRY

Page 183: Donald Harvey and Gene Williams, *Living in a Glass House: Surviving the Scrutiny of Ministry and Marriage* (Kansas City: Beacon Hill, 2002), as mentioned at: www.christianitytoday.com/ le/2002/004/31.101.html.

Page 186: Billy Graham, *Just As I Am: The Autobiography of Billy Graham* (San Francisco: HarperOne, 1997), 828.

Page 186: Ibid.

CHAPTER 11:
CAMP 3: INJECTING "DAD" IN EDUCATION

Page 192: J. C. Ryle, *Duties of Parents, Part 3*.

CHAPTER 12:
CAMP 4: PRODUCING TOMORROW'S DISCIPLES

Page 199: Mike DeVries, "Worshipping at the Altar of Me: The Role of Parents in Kids' Spiritual Formation." Posted 2003, www .youthspecialties.com/articles/topics/family/altar.php.

CHAPTER 13:
A VIEW FROM THE SUMMIT

Page 210: Caroline Alexander, "Murdering the Impossible," *National Geographic* (Nov. 2006), 62.

Page 210: Ibid., 67.

Page 217: C. S. Lewis, *The Screwtape Letters* (San Francisco: Harper-One, 2001), 162.

Page 219: A tip of the hat goes to cycling commentator Paul Sherwin for his colorful expression "reaching into his suitcase of courage."

Page 219: William Ebenstein, *Great Political Thinkers: Plato to the Present*, 4th ed. (New York: Holt, Rinehart, & Winston, 1969), 585.

Page 220: Jon Krakauer, *Into Thin Air*, 173.

Acknowledgments

An author's passion and vision alone do not publish a book. It takes considerable input, dialogue, and torch carrying from others to mold a raw idea and craft it into something that you can actually hold in your hands. I am grateful to so many who came along side me and participated in this vision.

My gratitude must begin with Don Pape. Besides my wife, Don was the initial torchbearer of the book and worked tirelessly to ensure that it came to life. I am also indebted to Angela Scheff and Michael Ranville at Zondervan, both of whom were instrumental in turning my vision into a published work.

I was blessed to be able to talk to many people in my research and get their insights on biblical fatherhood. Special thanks, in particular, go to Vince Lichlyter, Csaba Leidenfrost, and Sandi Horine for sharing their stories with me.

I am deeply appreciative of the critiques that Lori Vanden Bosch, Andy Meisenheimer, and Angela Scheff provided on the initial manuscript. Thanks also to Verlyn Verbrugge for his feedback and fine editorial eye on the final submission. All of their suggestions helped ensure that the text did not take unwanted detours or unnecessary sidetrips away from the core message of the book.

Finally, I am so ever thankful to Kim, my lovely wife, and my sons, Jordan, Jared, and Justus, for their unwavering encouragement and support. *ad alta simul*—to the summit, together.

STUDY GUIDE QUESTIONS

CHAPTER 1

1. Do you feel a deep yearning for adventure or a purpose? How is this need expressed in your life?

2. Which of the following are you most passionate about—your career, ministry, hobby, or recreational activity?

3. How much personal worth and purpose do you get from this activity (activities)? Does this activity (activities) ever conflict with your responsibilities at home?

4. Do you struggle with putting more priority with this activity than your family?

5. Do you identify with the Rugged Individualist, Expectations Guy, or Balanced Man? If so, which one?

6. Do you ever struggle with looking at your role as father/husband as "duty/obligation" rather than "opportunity"?

CHAPTER 2

1. Why is it easy for men to become seduced by their careers and allow them to take over their lives?

2. To what extent are your social, emotional, and personal needs met by your profession?

3. To what extent is your self-identity tied to your career? Is this biblical?

4. How much value does today's family place on the family as a whole versus individual pursuits? How would you gauge your family?

5. Have you ever lost perspective as Rich did in his work–family struggles?

CHAPTER 3

1. What mistakes did the fathers of Kendra and Adam make in raising their children? In hindsight, what should they have done differently?

2. What percentage of children raised in Christian homes leave their faith when they go to college? What are some of the reasons for these statistics?

3. Read Proverbs 22:6. To what extent is a father responsible for the faith of his children?

4. What is a "balanced life"? How can a man's need for adventure/purpose derail his quest for balance?

5. Is the goal of a balanced life really achievable in the real world? Why or why not?

Chapter 4

1. How does the role of an Everest expedition leader parallel the biblical role of a father? Describe each of the responsibilities.

2. Read Deuteronomy 6:6–9. What does this passage mean, practically speaking, for a father living in the twenty-first century?

3. How much of a problem are sibling rivalries, bickering, and bad attitudes in your family? Read Ephesians 6:4. What should your role be as a father in dealing with this sin?

4. What is a "family adventure" as described in the chapter? What is it *not*?

5. According to the chapter, what is the two-pronged "summit" that a family should work toward together? What obstacles do you face in making this happen in your family?

Chapter 5

1. Is breadwinning the primary responsibility of a man? Why or why not?

2. What tension do you have between providing for your family and spending time with them?

3. How can the Provider Dad mentality cause a man to downplay his responsibility of leading his family?

4. If both leading and providing for a family are critical, how does a man prioritize when they conflict? What is a biblical response?

5. What is a Peripheral Dad? How can a Provider Dad slip into being a Peripheral Dad?

CHAPTER 6

1. What are the four callings of a man? Do they complement or compete with each other? Explain.

2. Why must a man fully surrender his life to Christ in order to lead his family biblically?

3. Recount the stories of Müller and Taylor. How did they demonstrate their faith in a practical way?

4. Read Ephesians 4:1. How does this verse give insight into the sense of adventure and purpose that is buried deep inside a man?

5. Read Deuteronomy 6:5–7. Is hands-on leadership an option for fathers or is it essential?

6. Compare and contrast Noah and Eli as fathers. What fatal mistakes did Eli make in raising his boys?

Chapter 7

1. How does a man's window of opportunity in his career compete with his window with his kids?

2. Recount the story of Gordon Clune. Have you felt the tension he faced between career and his quickly growing kids? Are there steps you need to take to be sure that you do not make the same mistakes?

3. According to the statistics cited in the chapter, how can parental influence be so strong for adolescents, yet be forgotten about when these same kids leave home?

4. How can a man have "street cred" with his kids?

5. Do you have "street cred" in your family? If not, what steps can you take to gain it?

Chapter 8

1. What does it mean, practically speaking, to live as a modern-day disciple?

2. If "lip service" is a 0 and "total abandonment" is a 10, how would you rank your faith and trust in Jesus Christ? What steps can you take to move to a higher number?

3. Read James 1:3. Do we expect these times of testing in our lives? Should we?

4. Why is following Christ not a matter of cause-effect?

STUDY GUIDE QUESTIONS

235

5. According to the chapter, what is the power of the words "but if not"?

CHAPTER 9

1. How would you rate your own TAFF—Time Away From Family? Is all of that time necessary?

2. When should a man place his career "on hold" when his kids are growing up in his home? Give a couple of examples.

3. Read 1 Corinthians 3:18–20 and Proverbs 3:5–7. How can common sense be a tool used by God? How can it also be a tool used by Satan?

4. How significant of a barrier can common sense be to a man who wants to sacrifice career ambition for his family?

5. According to the chapter, what does "Christ sense" mean?

6. How can a man's family become a stumbling block to following Christ's call?

7. What limits do you need to place on your career when you have children living in your home?

CHAPTERS 10 AND 11

1. What are some of the benefits and downsides that a church ministry can have on a man's family?

2. A man's primary mission field is his family. Agree or disagree? Back up your answer with Scripture.

3. What can a man learn from the experiences of Billy Graham discussed in chapter 10?

4. What four steps should a man take to ensure his ministry does not trump his family commitment?

5. What role does education play in training up disciples?

6. What is a man's biblical role in educating his kids? How much responsibility does he have?

7. Why is a man's leadership in his children's education an important component to real biblical fatherhood?

CHAPTER 12

1. Read Matthew 28:19–20. How does the Great Commission provide a roadmap for a man discipling his kids?

2. What are the three stages of training children in their faith? How does a father's role change in each of these phases?

3. If you have kids in the home, what stage are they at? How do you need to respond?

4. Why is it critical for a man to establish a culture of discipleship in his house?

5. Read 1 Thessalonians 2:7–12. How does Paul provide a worthy example for how a man should guide his kids?

CHAPTER 13

1. What kind of legacy do you see yourself as leading at this point in your life? Are you pleased or heartbroken by what you see? What steps can you take to produce a lasting legacy with your kids?

2. What are some testing points a man will face when becoming an Expeditionary Man? What is your testing point? Be specific.

3. Is God calling you to a major change in your life in order to become the biblical man that God has called you to be?

4. What are some specific steps you can do to make it happen?

ABOUT
THE AUTHOR

Rich Wagner is author of *The Myth of Happiness, The Gospel Unplugged,* and several *For Dummies* books designed to make biblical truth easily approachable for postmodern readers. These books include *C. S. Lewis & Narnia for Dummies, Christianity for Dummies,* and *Christian Prayer for Dummies.* A former Silicon Valley entrepreneur, Rich was previously vice president of product development at an Internet software company. Rich lives in New England with his wife and three sons. He can be found online at *richwagnerwords.com.*

Share Your Thoughts

With the Author: Your comments will be forwarded to
the author when you send them to *zauthor@zondervan.com*.

With Zondervan: Submit your review of this book
by writing to *zreview@zondervan.com*.

Free Online Resources at
www.zondervan.com/hello

 Zondervan AuthorTracker: Be notified whenever your
favorite authors publish new books, go on tour, or post
an update about what's happening in their lives.

 Daily Bible Verses and Devotions: Enrich your life
with daily Bible verses or devotions that help you start
every morning focused on God.

 Free Email Publications: Sign up for newsletters on
fiction, Christian living, church ministry, parenting, and
more.

 Zondervan Bible Search: Find and compare
Bible passages in a variety of translations at
www.zondervanbiblesearch.com.

 Other Benefits: Register yourself to receive online
benefits like coupons and special offers, or to participate
in research.